The Battle OF
Harlem Heights,
1776

SMALL BATTLES

Mark Edward Lender and James Kirby Martin, Series Editors

The Battle of Gloucester, 1777
by Garry Wheeler Stone and Paul W. Schopp

The Battle of Musgrove's Mill, 1780
by John Buchanan

The Battle of Upper Sandusky, 1782
by Eric Sterner

The Battles of Connecticut Farms and Springfield, 1780
by Edward G. Lengel

The Battle OF Harlem Heights

1776

"The U.S. Army's First Victory and the
Legacy of Thomas Knowlton"

DAVID PRICE

SMALL
BATTLES

WESTHOLME
Yardley

Westholme Publishing, LLC
904 Edgewood Road
Yardley, Pennsylvania 19067
Visit our Web site at www.westholmepublishing.com

ISBN: 978-1-59416-394-4
Also available as an eBook.

Printed in the United States of America.

To the memory of my parents,
Irving Seymour Price and Norma Master Price

Good Officers is the very Soul of an Army; the activity and Zeal of the Troops entirely depends upon the degree of animation given them by their officers.

— Nathanael Greene to John Adams, June 2, 1776

Contents

Maps

A gallery of illustrations follows page 71

Series Editors' Introduction

WE ALL HAVE HEARD and likely read about the big battles of the American Revolution. Names like Trenton, Saratoga, and Yorktown resonate in our ears. But what about all the smaller battles that took place by the hundreds, often fought away from but related to the bigger battles. It is the contention of this series that these smaller actions, too often ignored, had as much impact, if not more, in shaping the outcomes of the American War of Independence.

These engagements were most often fought at the grassroots level. They did not directly involve His Majesty's professional forces under the likes of Generals William Howe, John Burgoyne, and Henry Clinton, or Continentals under Generals George Washington, Nathanael Greene, or Horatio Gates for that matter. Such smaller battles involved local forces, such as patriot militia and partisan bands of Loyalists, or at times Native Americans, mostly, but not always, fighting on the British side.

Quite often the big names were not there in such smaller-scale combat. Private Joseph Plumb Martin, writing in his classic memoir, recalled his fighting at Forts Mifflin and Mercer during November 1777. He and his comrades were trying to block British war and supply vessels moving up the Delaware River from reaching the king's troops under Sir William Howe who had captured Philadelphia. Had they prevailed and cut off this obvious supply route, Howe might well have had to abandon the city. But no, they did not succeed. Superior British firepower finally defeated these courageous American fighters.

What bothered Martin, besides so many good soldiers being seriously wounded or killed, was not the failed but valiant effort to cut off Howe's primary supply line. Rather, writing thirty years later, what particularly irked him was that "there has been but little notice taken of" this critical action. Martin was sure he knew why: "The reason of which is, there was no Washington, Putnam, or Wayne there. . . . Such [circumstances] and such troops generally get but little notice taken of them, do what they will. Great men get great praise, little men, nothing."

While Martin's blunt lament is unusual in the literature of the Revolution, the circumstances he described and complained of are actually fairly obvious. Although often brutal, the smaller engagements too frequently have received short shrift in popular narratives about the conflict. Nor have the consequences of these various actions been carefully studied in relation to the bigger battles and the outcomes of the War for Independence more generally. Small battles accounted for the lion's share of the combat that occurred during the American Revolution. The purpose of this series is to shine a bright new light on these smaller engagements while also getting to know those lesser persons who participated in them and grappling with the broader consequences and greater meaning of these actions on local, regional, and nation-making levels.

In the end, a more complete understanding of the Revolutionary War's big picture will emerge from the small-battles volumes that make up this series. If, as recent scholarship tells us, local history "allows us to peer deep into past societies and to see their very DNA," the Small Battles Series will do the same for the American War of Independence.

The Battle of Harlem Heights, 1776 is the fourth title in the Small Battles Series, and we are very pleased to recommend it. Author

David Price, a long-time historical interpreter at Washington Crossing Historic Park and author of a fine book on Second Trenton, has taken advantage of original new research and the most recent literature to give us a fresh perspective on the action at Harlem Heights. Fought on September 16, 1776, the battle was a bright spot for the rebels in the midst of Washington's losing campaign to hold New York City for the revolutionary cause. Price deals concisely with the events of the day, offering a clear analysis of how and why patriot leadership was able to take advantage of British overconfidence and land a stinging check on William Howe's advance against the retreating American army. Brief as it was, however, Price sees real significance in the engagement: Even as Washington's forces were pulling back in the face of Howe's assault, rebel forces displayed considerable tactical acumen, and patriot commanders, far from despairing, sought opportunities to strike at the King's troops. In the face of real adversity, Harlem Heights signaled that the patriot army remained operational and dangerous, and David Price has given us an outstanding account of this genuinely interesting and important small battle.

Mark Edward Lender
James Kirby Martin
Series editors

Introduction

THE BATTLE OF HARLEM HEIGHTS is a notable, if largely unappreciated, milestone in American military history. This engagement on upper Manhattan Island in September 1776 marked the first successful battlefield outcome achieved by George Washington's troops in the War of Independence. It also portended the gradual emergence of a proficient fighting force among the citizen-soldiers who comprised the Continental Army that Washington led and which bore the brunt of a young nation's quest for political and economic self-determination against Great Britain.

Henry P. Johnston's classic study, *The Battle of Harlem Heights, September 16, 1776*, published in 1897, has traditionally been regarded as the seminal work on this subject, and the volume before you makes considerable use of Johnston's scholarship, as well as more recent studies of the battle and the 1776 New York campaign of which it was a part. The latter include, in particular, Bruce Bliven, Jr.'s *Battle for Manhattan* (1956) and Barnet Schecter's *The Battle for New York: The City at the Heart of the American Revolution* (2002), two very estimable histories that in turn owe a considerable debt to Johnston's labors.

That said, it is time for a new look at the Harlem Heights encounter. This work represents an effort to combine sound scholarship with a fresh perspective on a little-known event, one that conveys an enhanced appreciation of the battle and also seeks to raise the historical profile of a key participant who is largely unknown outside the ranks of Revolutionary War aficionados. Colonel Thomas Knowlton of Connecticut was mortally wounded in this affray while leading an elite contingent known as Knowlton's Rangers, the U.S. Army's first intelligence and reconnaissance unit. Knowlton and his Rangers precipitated and were especially conspicuous in the engagement, and the extensive focus on him and the men he led lends this new literary endeavor a distinctive quality. While a limited amount of information may be found about Knowlton in a wide variety of primary and secondary sources, to the author's knowledge no single modern-day work has incorporated this level of detail about the colonel's life and his record in the Revolution. The attention paid here to Knowlton as a military figure, and especially as the father of American military intelligence, is long overdue.

It must be conceded that the American victory at Harlem Heights provided little more than a temporary spur in morale for the rebel cause in 1776, a momentary respite from what was otherwise an unrelenting series of reversals suffered by a ragtag army during its near-disastrous New York campaign. This engagement did nothing to alter the direction of that campaign or the military events immediately following. The stiff resistance offered by Washington's troops on that occasion probably contributed to a brief delay in the offensive launched by the Anglo-German army commanded by General William Howe, which had prior to September 16 claimed two easy victories over the Americans, at the Battle of Long Island (otherwise known as the Battle of Brooklyn) on August 27 and when the Crown's soldiery landed at Kip's Bay on Manhattan Island's eastern shore on September 15. The determined stand made by the rebels at Harlem Heights constituted an unexpected show of force against the redcoats and their German allies (known to Americans as Hessians), who had become accustomed to seeing the backs of the American defenders in full flight. However, given General Howe's cautious manner and the strong defensive position occupied by Washington's units on the Harlem bluffs, one cannot be confident that Howe would have pursued the Americans any more aggressively than he did had there been no fighting at Harlem Heights.

When it comes to the significance of the clash on September 16, 1776, what can be said with a reasonable degree of confidence is that it provided valuable, even crucial, combat experience for an inexperienced and ill-trained army of rebellion attempting to fend off an invasion by a foe that was better trained, disciplined, and equipped, and more experienced—especially among its senior officer corps. With that came a newfound realization among the Continental soldiers that they could, under the right circumstances, effectively oppose the enemy, although this greater confidence would be sorely tested in the weeks following the events at Harlem Heights. Howe's army completed its triumphant New York campaign in November 1776 and invaded New Jersey, while Washington's battered force abandoned most of the latter and sought refuge on the Pennsylvania side of the Delaware River.

Perhaps the most significant attribute of the Battle of Harlem Heights is that it provided a harbinger of what was to come for the army that embodied the Revolutionary cause—the development of a fighting force in which soldiers from different regions would learn how to do battle and gain a greater sense of national identity in regard to the cause for which they were fighting. On September 16, 1776, New Englanders, Marylanders, and Virginians waged war together in a successful action for the first time. Prior to the rebellion, these men, along with the vast majority of their fellow Americans, would have identified themselves by their colony of residence rather than as citizens of a sovereign nation separate and apart from their mother country England. As the war progressed, the hardcore veterans of Washington's army gained an enhanced degree of national consciousness, a perspective not necessarily shared by the civilian population who had been spared the harsh realities of combat and camp life.

In the end, the affair at Harlem Heights had little, if any, short-term impact on the course of the war but contributed to the development of a fighting spirit and a greater sense of interregional cohesion among Washington's soldiers. For the British and Hessians, it was easy to dismiss the import of what occurred there since at the end of the day, no ground had changed hands. Still, the battle must have made an impression on at least some of the Crown's men given that the resistance they encountered was very different from what they had faced to that point, even from what had been demonstrated the day before when they chased the defenders up Manhattan Island with ease after landing at Kip's Bay. Although General Howe's estimate of British and Hessian casualties in this clash was typically understated, those among his officers who knew the extent of their losses, which were perhaps three times that of the Americans, may very well have discerned the portents of a new and disquieting military reality—that the task of suppressing the rebellion might prove far more challenging than they had expected.

ONE

An Unequal Contest

TAKING COMMAND

George Washington was the obvious choice when in June 1775 the Continental Congress appointed a commander-in-chief of the new American army being assembled from the armed colonials gathered outside Boston. As a Southerner and resident of the largest colony, Virginia, it was hoped his selection would generate support beyond New England for the colonial rebellion against Great Britain. In addition, the forty-three-year-old planter from the Old Dominion had a highly regarded military record as a young colonel in the French and Indian War and had demonstrated as a Virginia legislator and delegate to both the First and Second Continental Congress his appreciation for the nuances of government and politics. Furthermore, Washington looked the part of a commander and exhibited temperance, earnestness, and prudence—all of which enhanced his dignified and imposing presence.[1]

The original Revolutionary army of citizen-soldiers, which gathered around Boston after hostilities erupted at Lexington and Concord in April 1775 and was nominally commanded by General Artemas Ward of Massachusetts, conspicuously lacked cohesion. The men from Connecticut, New Hampshire, and Rhode Island, who had come to the aid of their Massachusetts brethren, were each under independent control and voluntarily yielded to General Ward's authority. The appointment of Washington as commander-in-chief and the adoption by Congress of these troops as the Continental Army, operating under the orders and in the pay of Congress, imparted more of a military character to this collection of amateur warriors; however, the terms of enlistment were short and it would become necessary to reorganize the entire army by providing for new enlistments for a year's service effective January 1, 1776.[2]

Upon assuming command of the Continental Army on July 2, 1775, Washington had to organize the independent-minded rank and file, mostly New Englanders, whose egalitarian instincts led to disorder and indiscipline.[3] Washington brought a substantial measure of order to a frighteningly inept rabble, as he fervently believed in the importance of discipline to any military organization.[4] Aside from their lack of discipline and organizational structure, the troops Washington inherited had no common national identity and regarded themselves not as American nationals but residents of their individual colonies. And there were the recurring challenges of supply procurement—especially military equipment, gunpowder, and uniforms—and manpower shortages.

While trying to create an organized army, Washington achieved one noteworthy success against His Majesty's forces in the early months of the war without fighting a battle. In March 1776, he outmaneuvered General William Howe's garrison in Boston by placing artillery on Dorchester Heights that rebel forces had dragged overland from captured Fort Ticonderoga in upstate New York, thereby rendering the redcoats' position untenable. Still, Howe's evacuation of Boston on March 17 was one he had been planning for months, having received an order the previous November "to abandon that town before winter, and to move the army to New-York, or to some other place to the southward."[5] The British army's commander sought more advantageous ground on which to operate and awaited the arrival of a fleet that could accommodate his troops and those among the city's Loyalists who wished to depart. Once Howe had transported these civilians to Halifax, Nova Scotia, he prepared for an offensive against New York. A larger and more significant port city than Boston, its location at the base of the strategic Hudson River route to Lake Champlain made it the linchpin of any plan to take control of the Hudson River Valley. Capturing New York would, at least in theory, enable the British to isolate New England from the other colonies and force it to submit.

DEFENDING NEW YORK

At the beginning of 1776, Congress and General Washington made General Charles Lee responsible for defending New York. Formerly a British army officer and now the Americans' most experienced general, Lee ascended from third- to second-ranking officer of the Continental Army upon the resignation of Washington's original second-in-command, Artemas Ward. It was impossible to adequately fortify a seaport that had once relied upon the Royal Navy for its security but now faced the reality of being surrounded by accessible routes for an invasion borne by that same navy, with no rebel fleet to oppose it. Nevertheless, Lee conceived elaborate plans for a system of fortifications in lower Manhattan, Brooklyn Heights, and Paulus Hook (Jersey City today), and along the East River, together with a pair of strongholds high above the Hudson River: Fort Washington at the upper end of Manhattan and Fort Lee on the Jersey Palisades opposite.

Washington arrived in Manhattan on April 13, having come down from Boston after expelling General Howe's occupying force. He was no longer besieging a compact city but defending an area that extended over three islands and included a major harbor. The difficulty of doing so was compounded by the complexion of the Patriot forces. (As used in this narrative, the term

"Patriot" refers to those Americans who opposed British colonial policy in the years leading up to the outbreak of the Revolutionary War and actively supported, or at least expressed sympathy with, the effort made to secure the colonies' independence from Great Britain, as distinguished from the term "Loyalist," which refers to the colonists who supported British policy or at least opposed the quest for independence and desired to remain within the British Empire as subjects of the Crown and Parliament. American Patriots were sometimes referred to as "Whigs" and "Loyalists" as Tories, analogous to the opposing political factions in eighteenth-century Britain where the Whigs were generally considered more reform-minded than the Tories and the latter more aligned with the Crown.) Although Washington had about twenty thousand men under his command, comprising regiments from ten different states, fewer than half were Continental regulars.[6] He set his troops to work building fortifications, initially based on Lee's plan—including extensive entrenchments on Brooklyn Heights to defend against both naval and ground attacks—and then adopted major modifications that featured barricades and batteries in New York City itself, facing both the Hudson and East Rivers.

The city of twenty thousand—larger than Boston but smaller than Philadelphia and in peacetime a center of commerce, shipbuilding, and trade—was less than a square mile and covered not even a tenth of Manhattan Island (about thirteen miles long and a little over two miles wide at its widest point), then known as New York Island or York Island. The rest of this isle, then referred to as the Outward, bristled with woods, streams, marshes, and stretches of rocky terrain, and was sprinkled with a few small farms and imposing country estates, all the way to its northern tip at King's Bridge on the Harlem River. Here a narrow wooden bridge linked the island to Westchester County on the mainland.[7]

The British ministry's resolve to swiftly crush the colonial uprising in 1776 was embodied by the armada it sent across the Atlantic, with over four hundred ships bearing 1,200 cannon and carrying thirty-two thousand soldiers and ten thousand sailors.

This undertaking exceeded any amphibious operation by a European nation to that point, with an attack force greater than the population of Philadelphia, then the largest city in America.[8] When the fleet began appearing in New York's lower harbor at the end of June, it seemed to one American observer that "all London was afloat."[9]

On July 1, the British army landed on Staten Island and encamped there while awaiting reinforcements. The latter included nine thousand Hessians, who arrived in mid-August, along with a smaller force under Lieutenant General Henry Clinton, the son of a former Royal Governor of New York, coming up from the Southern theater after an unsuccessful attack on Charleston, South Carolina. Clinton grew up in America, joined the British army at age fifteen, and saw action in many campaigns during the War of Austrian Succession (1740–1748) and the Seven Years' War (1756–1763). He was promoted to general in 1772 and returned to America in May 1775 with General Howe and General John Burgoyne. After General Thomas Gage returned to England in October 1775, Clinton became second in command to Howe.

The Hessians were soldiers from the small states of Germany, then the largest suppliers of troops on earth.[10] The princes of a half-dozen such states had hired out their soldiers to fight for George III against the American rebellion in early 1776. In contrast with its unrivaled naval power, England's relatively small army was unable by itself to defeat this uprising and at the same time protect the British Isles and the rest of the empire—a reflection of the traditional aversion among the English people to a large standing army that might be put to tyrannical use. About two-thirds of the German soldiers who crossed the Atlantic were from Hesse-Cassel and Hesse-Hanau, mostly the former. Although they alone were technically "Hessians," Americans applied that name to all the German soldiers. Notwithstanding the popular impression to the contrary, it can be argued that these men were not "mercenaries" as the term is commonly understood because Britain paid each prince for his soldiers' services rather than directly compensating the soldiers.

The Crown's troops settled into their Staten Island encampment as they prepared for a campaign carefully planned by General Howe and his older brother, Admiral Richard Lord Howe, who commanded the fleet that dominated the waters around New York. The Howe brothers were officers of high ability with substantial wartime experience.[11] Moreover, they had at their disposal the might and majesty of the Royal Navy, in addition to a modern professional land force—if modest in size—that had an unparalleled record of victory in its recent service. From 1755 to 1764, Britain's army had fought successfully on five continents. Its generals averaged thirty years of military service in contrast to two years for their American counterparts, and its privates averaged nine years of service as compared with the few months of active duty most rebel enlistees had at this stage in the war.[12]

Considering the disadvantages the defending army faced, any serious plan to resist an invasion of Manhattan or Long Island was arguably doomed from a military standpoint, and therefore the attempt to hold New York City was based on political more than military considerations. The loss of America's second largest city without a reasonably determined effort at defending it would presumably dishearten Congress and the Patriot faction among the civilian population. Washington wishfully suggested to the president of Congress, John Hancock, that the enemy's confidence and that of their Loyalist sympathizers was misplaced: "I trust through divine favor and our own exertions they will be disappointed in their views, and at all events any Advantages they may gain will cost them very dear."[13]

THE ARMIES PREPARE

William Howe, third son of the second Viscount Howe and the forty-seven-year-old commander of the British land forces in America, was an able and personally courageous officer who had joined the military at age eighteen, served with distinction during the French and Indian War, and become one of Britain's leading officers even before being promoted to major general in 1772. He was fortunate to face an opposing army deficient in experience, training, and equipment, whereas he led the most powerful expedition Britain had ever sent beyond Europe and the largest it had deployed anywhere for several decades.[14]

The Howe brothers' first tactical move was to demonstrate the futility of resisting the king's naval prowess. On July 12, five warships sailed from Staten Island past the lower tip of Manhattan and up the Hudson with guns blazing, damaging several private residences while sustaining barely a scratch from the onshore batteries. This occurred even as ardent Patriots celebrated their newly declared separation from the mother country—"an appeal to the tribunal of the world" declared by Congress on July 4.[15] The Royal Navy's incursion provided a vivid reminder that the Crown and its armed forces would not easily concede the independence of a people they regarded as deluded subjects. According to Ambrose Serle, Admiral Howe's private secretary, the action by Congress proclaimed "the Villainy & the Madness of these deluded People. . . . A more impudent, false and atrocious Proclamation was never fabricated by the Hands of Man."[16] The naval exhibition followed by three days the actions of a city mob, inspired by Congress's declaration, to topple the equestrian statue of George III on Bowling Green. Its lead contents would be repurposed, according to Lieutenant Isaac Bangs of Massachusetts, "to be run up into Musquet Balls for the use of the Yankies."[17]

Reflecting his inexperience as an army commander and largely disregarding General Lee's original plan of defense, Washington committed a cardinal strategic sin when he scattered his units in the face of a larger and superior foe. He allocated seven brigades to lower Manhattan—including two each along the Hudson and East Rivers, one inside the city, and two in reserve—with two at Fort Washington and King's Bridge in northern Manhattan, two on Long Island, and two on Governors Island below Manhattan. The British encouraged this troop dispersion by dispatching small forces to harass the defenders at various locations.[18]

As summer passed, sickness spread among the rebel ranks from several sources: malnutrition from a lack of fresh food and green vegetables; venereal disease from encounters with local prostitutes; and gastrointestinal maladies—dysentery, typhoid, malaria, and intestinal ailments—from poor sanitation practices by inexperienced and undisciplined enlistees, which led to polluted encampments and a contaminated water supply. Major General Nathanael Greene reported to Washington in July "that a putrid fever prevailed in my Brigade and . . . I thought it partly oweing to their feeding too freely on animal food. Vegetables would be much more wholesome."[19]

Greene, only thirty-four when the war started and the product of a prominent Rhode Island family, had deviated from his Quaker roots to embrace the army and impressed the commander-in-chief with his talent for organizational efficiency, which earned him command of the troops on Long Island. Indeed, Washington was convinced that if he was killed or captured, Greene was best qualified among his generals to succeed him.[20] However, the young Rhode Islander was stricken with a fever in late summer, and Washington named Major General John Sullivan to replace him on August 20. Sullivan was a thirty-six-year-old attorney from New Hampshire and a former delegate to the first Continental Congress who became a brigadier general in June 1775 and a major general in August 1776. Regrettably, Sullivan was unfamiliar with the ground he was assigned to defend and lacked Greene's ability and judgment.[21] On August 24, Washington replaced him with fifty-eight-year-old Major General Israel Putnam, a lionized veteran of the French and Indian War who was brave and popular with the troops and had a better knowledge of Long Island than Sullivan. "Old Put," however, lacked the experience and temperament to command a force of several thousand soldiers.[22]

Having three different generals in charge on Long Island over five days made for a confused command system just when such disruption would likely have its most unfortunate repercussions, for controlling Long Island was essential to defending New York. On August 22, some fifteen thousand redcoats and fifteen hundred Hessians with forty cannon landed on the beaches of Gravesend Bay along the island's southern shore, followed by more than four thousand Hessians three days later. They comprised more than 90 percent of General Howe's total force, but the reports arriving at Washington's headquarters indicated that only about nine thousand enemy troops had landed on Long Island. Faulty intelligence compelled Washington to make decisions about the disposition of his soldiery with inadequate knowledge of where Howe's units were, and he hesitated to act without knowing where his opponent would strike.[23] Until the day of battle, the American commander remained doubtful as to whether the British intended to throw their entire weight against his Long Island defenses or simultaneously send a division up the Hudson River to attack upper Manhattan.[24]

Writing on August 26 from his headquarters in New York City to the manager of his Mount Vernon estate, cousin Lund Washington, the commander-in-chief admitted his ignorance of British intentions in the wake of their landing "a pretty considerable part of their force" on Long Island: "What their real design is I know not; whether they think our works round this City are too strong, and have a Mind to bend their whole force that way—or whether it is intended as a feint—or is to form part of their Attack, we cannot as yet tell."[25] Washington and his senior officers even lacked reliable information about how many rebel troops were actually on Long Island. The estimates have run from 9,450 to 11,000 men, serving in a total of between sixteen and thirty-one regiments.[26]

Although Washington suspected that Howe's landing on Long Island was a feint to shift his attention away from an assault on Manhattan, he did send reinforcements to support the nearly six thousand men already posted across the East River. Unfortunately, Washington committed another blunder by ordering thirteen senior officers to leave their commands at a critical moment and remain in Manhattan on August 25 and 26 to sit as a court-martial of Lieutenant Colonel Herman Zedwitz, a Continental officer from Prussia apprehended while attempting to sell American intelligence to British officers for two thousand pounds. The court-martial sat so late on August 26—Zedwitz was found guilty and cashiered from the army—that it was impossible for these officers to cross the East River that day. When they finally rejoined their regiments, the battle for Long Island was already in progress.

Across the East River, General Howe's troops had settled into camp in and around the village of Flatbush, forming a line along the base of the ridge that rose across Long Island, as their commanders reconnoitered the terrain. Flatbush was one of a half-dozen townships, along with Brooklyn, Bushwick, Flatlands, Gravesend, and New Utrecht, which made up the pastoral setting of King's County (the borough of Brooklyn today), with Brooklyn being farthest to the northwest and encompassing Brooklyn Heights. The heavily wooded ridge north of Flatbush, known as the Gowanus Heights, stretched laterally for nearly three miles across the island south of the American fortifications in Brooklyn. To reach those rebel defenses, the king's forces would have to penetrate one or more of four passes through the sloping landscape, from west to east: Gowanus Road, Flatbush Road, Bedford Pass, and Jamaica Pass.

Henry Clinton's reconnaissance provided Howe with the key to victory, a testament to the former's status as the most cerebral of His Majesty's generals in America.[27] Having discovered the Jamaica Pass was unprotected, he proposed a daring night march along this easternmost route through the Gowanus ridge to turn Putnam's flank and drive the Americans back to Brooklyn Heights. Howe agreed to the plan, notwithstanding his reluctance to follow any recommendation from Clinton, whom he considered overbearing and transparently ambitious.[28] It was the first and last time Howe would do so.[29] Putnam apparently considered the Jamaica Pass too remote to pose a threat and left it guarded by only five mounted militia officers with four hundred Pennsylvanians posted along the road between that pass and the Bedford Pass three miles to the west. The three passes that were defended were too distant from each other for those guarding them to reinforce each other if attacked, making Old Put's line along the Gowanus Heights dangerously vulnerable.[30]

A NEAR DISASTER

The Battle of Long Island began on the Americans' right shortly after midnight on August 27, when Pennsylvania riflemen fired at a party of redcoats foraging in a watermelon patch. The real action would not occur until daybreak. General Howe led half his army—ten thousand men with eighteen cannon—along back roads and up the Jamaica Pass according to Clinton's plan. They were still marching at sunrise when his other two divisions launched a diversionary attack; a British force under Major General James Grant struck the rebel right near Gowanus Bay and Hessian troops under Lieutenant General Leopold von Heister hit their center at Flatbush. No doubt, Grant viewed this engagement as an opportunity to end the misguided notion of a sovereign American nation at one blow, having written that "if a good bleeding can bring these Bible-faced Yankees to their senses—the fever of Independence should soon abate."[31]

The British advance north along the Gowanus Road prompted Putnam to order Brigadier General William Alexander, known as Lord Stirling, and his brigade with the elite Maryland and Delaware regiments into action at three a.m. (Stirling, a New York native, claimed to have inherited a Scottish earldom, which was upheld in the Scottish courts but rejected by the British House of Lords. An almost-fifty-year-old merchant with an estate in Basking Ridge, New Jersey, he grew up well-educated with a large inheritance but ardently supported the Revolution, becoming a New Jersey militia colonel in 1775 and being promoted to general in March 1776.) By dawn, the brigade's two thousand men faced an enemy force of five thousand, and reinforcements swelled the latter's ranks to nine thousand as Stirling suffered mounting casualties.

Washington crossed the East River by eight a.m. and observed the unfolding battle through a spyglass from the fortifications at Brooklyn Heights. Howe's column discharged two cannon at nine a.m. to announce its arrival at Bedford Village and signal his other forces on the south side of the Gowanus Heights that the flanking movement had reached its objective. With the enemy applying pressure from the south and cutting off any retreat to the east or north, the rebels' outer defenses disintegrated. Their left and center swiftly collapsed, and those who could fled to the redoubts on Brooklyn Heights. By ten a.m., Washington's army was hopelessly outflanked and the enemy converged around Stirling's brigade.

The Maryland and Delaware regiments halted the British long enough for other American units to elude the attackers; however, Stirling realized he could not hold his position much longer. British troops blocked any retreat along the Gowanus Road, and that left only one means of escape—swimming across the Gowanus Creek at its widest on his right rear with the tide flowing in. While the rest of his brigade did just that, Stirling with nearly four hundred Marylanders gave the others cover by charging up the Gowanus Road against the Crown's troops in their rear. The latter were led by Lieutenant General Charles Earl Cornwallis, the most aristocratic of His Majesty's generals serving in America and one of the few British officers to study at a military academy. The thirty-seven-year-old Cornwallis, who came from a family noted for its military tradition, obtained a commission in the 1st Regiment of Foot Guards at age eighteen. An Eton College graduate and member of the House of Lords from his early twenties, he became a lieutenant colonel at age twenty-three and witnessed considerable military action in European wars before arriving in America in February 1776. Holding off the enemy long enough to allow the remainder of his command to make it to safety, Stirling surrendered himself to General von Heister rather than yield to the British directly. Just seven of those crossing the creek were lost by drowning, but some 250 of the Marylanders accompanying Stirling died in the fighting at the nearby Cortelyou House and more than a hundred were wounded or captured. Only ten men out of the 250 made it back to the American lines.[32]

No military engagement of the Revolution was larger than this—forty thousand men were involved if naval personnel are counted—and few had a more one-sided result.[33] Howe's attack produced the most brilliant tactical success achieved by the British on any Revolutionary War battlefield.[34] Still, he had failed to destroy the rebel army as about half the defenders involved in the fighting escaped. Delaware Lieutenant Enoch Anderson was somber but mildly hopeful: "A hard day this, for us poor Yankees! Superior discipline and numbers had overcome us. A gloomy time it was, but we solaced ourselves that at another time we

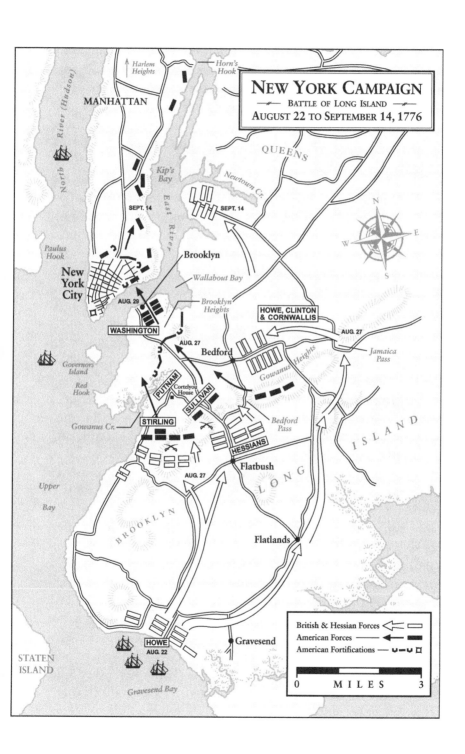

should do better."[35] The Americans figured their losses at about three hundred killed and 1,100 captured, with no reliable estimates of the wounded.[36] Their official casualty counts were probably very conservative and imprecise at best.[37] The British counted just under four hundred casualties: sixty-one redcoat fatalities, 267 wounded, and thirty-one captured or missing, along with Hessian losses of two dead and twenty-six wounded.[38]

The profusion of errors by Washington in his first major battle as commanding general had nearly disastrous repercussions. He was fighting a superior foe with only 50 percent of his strength because half his men were in Manhattan, and after Nathanael Greene took ill had changed commanders on Long Island twice in one week just before the battle. Worst of all, leaving the Jamaica Pass unguarded exposed the army's left to a flanking move that would have been catastrophic if not for herculean resistance by Stirling's brigade. The commander-in-chief was fortunate the British halted their drive toward Brooklyn Heights rather than forcing the Americans up against the East River. Perhaps recalling the carnage he had witnessed during his pyrrhic victory at Bunker Hill more than a year before, General Howe eschewed a frontal assault on the Patriot works for fear a direct attack would be just as costly and instead opted to lay siege to the Brooklyn lines, confident his brother's fleet would prevent the rebels escaping to Manhattan. Had he taken the advice of Clinton and others to storm those entrenchments, he would in all probability have succeeded.[39]

Washington despaired of the army's morale to President Hancock: "Our situation is truly distressing—The check our Detachment sustained on the 27th Ulto, has dispirited too great a proportion of our Troops and filled their minds with apprehension and despair." He complained that large numbers of militia were deserting: "Great numbers of them have gone off; in some Instances, almost by whole Regiments—by half Ones & by Companies at a time."[40] The opponent's perspective was perhaps best expressed by Ambrose Serle: "The Rebels abandoned every Spot as fast, I should say faster, than the King's Troops advanced upon them. . . . the Troops both British & Hessian . . . [i]n one thing only . . . failed—they could not run so fast as their Foes, many of whom were ready to run over each other."[41]

AFTER THE BATTLE

Following their setback at Long Island, Washington and his commanders realized they were in danger of having half the army trapped. They had been granted a momentary reprieve by General Howe's decision not to storm "the works constructed upon the heights of Brooklyn" on the 27th. He feared a direct frontal assault would entail an enormous cost—up to 1,500 Anglo-German dead or wounded—and assumed that he could take those fortifications by siege with far fewer casualties, or as he put it, "the lines must have been ours at a cheap rate, by regular approaches."[42] If the Continental troops remained on Brooklyn Heights, Howe's army would squeeze the noose around them while the Royal Navy cut off any escape.

Fortune smiled on the defenders when high winds prevented British warships from moving up the East River just prior to and during the battle, as did a storm that hovered for two days afterward. At a rebel council of war on August 29, the Continental generals decided to abandon Brooklyn beginning at eight p.m. that night. Darkness, followed by a thick fog at dawn, cloaked the withdrawal of virtually the entire American force and most of its stores across the East River near where the Brooklyn Bridge stands today. By seven a.m. on the 30th, small craft had ferried 9,500 soldiers, their horses, and most of their equipment to Manhattan. Washington rescued all but five of his cannon and left with the last of the troops.[43] Long Island was lost, but he had saved the army by an adroit maneuver that arguably compensated for his faulty judgment in the days preceding the battle. It ranks as one of the most skillful evacuations in military history, performed at night in small boats on a difficult waterway and eluding a numerically larger enemy and its potent fleet.[44]

The Continentals' commander-in-chief understood he could not hold New York City, at least not with the forces who had been routed on August 27, and risked entrapment if his troops did not seek more defensible ground. He confessed to John Hancock on September 2, "Till of late I had no doubt in my mind of defending this place nor should I have yet if the Men would do their duty, but this I despair of."[45] Washington's next missive to Hancock on September 8 discerned his adversary's intentions: "It is now extremely obvious from all Intelligence—from their movements, & every other circumstance that having landed their whole Army on Long Island (except about 4,000 on Staten Island) they mean to inclose us on the island of New York by taking post in our Rear, while the Shipping effectually secure the Front."[46]

Washington had again split his forces. He left some in lower Manhattan while awaiting authorization from Congress for the army to abandon New York City and posted the rest further north at Harlem Heights and Fort Washington, and above them at King's Bridge—the northernmost point of Manhattan. Ambrose Serle noted in his journal on September 2, "A great Part of their Army has left New York, and retired towards King's bridge, and farther back into the Country. Nothing terrifies these people more than the Apprehension of being surrounded. They will not fight at any Rate, unless they are sure of a Retreat."[47]

Delaware Colonel John Haslet, writing to his friend and political mentor Caesar Rodney two days after the army's evacuation from Brooklyn Heights, perceived an existential threat from British naval supremacy in the waters surrounding Manhattan Island: "I fear we shall be out numbered, expect every moment Orders to March off to King's Bridge, to prevent the Enemy Crossing the East River & confining us on another Nook. What the Event will be, God knows. . . . If the enemy can coop us up in N. York by Intrenching from River to River, horrid will be the Consequence from their Command of the Rivers."[48]

Nathanael Greene had recovered from the illness that caused Washington to relieve him of command a week before the Long Island battle, and he urged the commander-in-chief to abandon Manhattan Island and adopt a scorched earth policy in the process. Washington's youngest general argued that a prompt withdrawal from the island was "the only Eligible plan to oppose the Enemy successfully and secure ourselves from disgrace. I think we have no object on this side of Kings Bridge. Our Troops are now so scattered that one part may be cut off before the others can come to their support." Greene opined "that a General and speedy Retreat is absolutely necessary and that the honnor and interest of America requires it. I would burn the City and Subburbs . . . [to] deprive the Enemy of an opportunity of Barracking their whole Army together . . . [and] of a general Market."[49]

Washington spurned Greene's advice to torch New York although he clearly took it under consideration: "If we should be obliged to abandon this Town, ought it to stand as Winter Quarters for the Enemy? They would derive great conveniences from It on the one hand—and much property would be destroyed on the other—It is an important question, but will admit of but little time for deliberation."[50] Congress was loath to acquiesce in the destruction of a city it had insisted on defending against all odds. Ultimately the army's commander deferred to legislative guidance on this matter, as he did generally throughout the war, reflecting his deep-seated belief in the supremacy of civilian authority over the military.

The thought of abandoning New York may have been as demoralizing to Washington and his senior officers as the idea of reducing it to ashes, for it took them twelve days of intermittent debate in councils of war to reach the unavoidable decision to withdraw all their troops to northern Manhattan.[51] As the commander-in-chief explained, the faction advocating "a total and immediate removal from the City, urging the great danger of One part of the Army being cut off before the other can support It," had to overcome the objections of those "who thought for the present a large part of our force might be kept here and attempt to maintain the City a while longer."[52]

While these deliberations delayed the inevitable evacuation of the city, General Howe laid plans for a follow-up strike, making what he termed "the necessary preparations, and erecting batteries, to facilitate the landing upon the island of New-York."[53] These efforts included the positioning of landing craft for a Manhattan invasion, alluded to in Ambrose Serle's journal entry of September 7: "Great Preparations have been making all this Day; and about 80 Flatbottomed Boats were made ready for a further Debarkation of troops, and for a further attack upon the Rebels."[54]

Captain Frederick MacKenzie of the Royal Welch Fusiliers (the elite 23rd Regiment of Foot, an infantry unit formed in 1689 and primarily recruited in North Wales) noted in his diary on the 9th, "Everything indicates that we shall soon attempt something decisive against the Rebels, but considering the nature of the shore at Hellgate (Hell Gate on upper Manhattan's eastern shore) and rapidity of the tides and variety of eddies there, I do not suppose the landing will be made in that place. It appears probable that the erecting batteries against the enemy's works at Hellgate, and making so much demonstration there, is intended to draw their attention from some other point, for owing to the situation and construction of their principal work, it is extremely difficult to destroy it effectually." Rather than directly assaulting the Americans entrenched on the upper island's high ground, MacKenzie expected that "we shall land somewhere about Haerlem [Harlem], and by taking a position across the island, which is narrow in that part, endeavor to cut off all that part of the rebel army between us and New York."[55]

MacKenzie's estimate of the landing spot would be off by a considerable distance. On the 11th, British troops landed on Montresor's Island and Buchanan's Island (today conjoined islands known as Randall's Island and Wards Island) at the mouth of the Harlem River that separated upper Manhattan Island from the mainland, with the intention of using these as a springboard to cross over to Harlem and advance upon the city from the north. However, Washington had anticipated this move by withdrawing most of his forces to Harlem, and, as the potent American battery at Horn's Hook (near Eighty-ninth Street and East End Avenue today) had not been silenced, General Howe opted to land at Kip's Bay (the site of Thirty-fourth Street today).[56]

On the 13th, Ambrose Serle reported that four men-of-war were moving into position for an assault: "In the afternoon, the *Phoenix*, Capt. Parker, of 44 guns, the *Orpheus* of 32 guns, Capt. Hudson, the *Carysfort* of 28 guns, Capt. Fanshaw, and the *Roebuck* of 44 guns, Capt. Hammond, sailed up the East River to Bushwyck [Bushwick] Bay. . . . It was a fine Sight, if one could have divested one's Thoughts of the melancholy Reflection, that some Fellow-Creatures Lives were either taking away or in Danger, on account of the Villainy of the Rebel Leaders & Abettors."[57] Serle's journal entry the following day conveyed further news of the gathering force: "Five Transports sailed up the East River this Evening to join the Man of War, who went up last night," in addition to the four referenced above.[58] They would be joined by another transport the morning of the landing.

General Howe's orders of the 13th appealed to his men's martial spirits and their proficiency in the use of cold steel: "An attack upon the enemy being shortly intended, the soldiers are reminded of their evident superiority on the 27th August, by charging the rebels with their bayonets even in woods where they had thought themselves invincible." He recommended "to the troops an entire dependence upon their bayonets, with which they will ever command that success which their bravery so well deserves."[59]

The Continental troops awaiting Howe's next move were suffering from low morale, a lack of discipline and organization, and shortages of every kind.[60] On the eve of the invasion, Colonel Joseph Reed, the army's adjutant general (chief administrative officer), imparted ominous tidings to his wife: "The enemy are evidently intending to encompass us on this Island by a grand military exertion, which if successful must immortalize the name of Howe, to get this whole army and its stores in their power. I hope they will fail. It is now a trial of skill whether they shall or not, and every night we lie down with the most anxious fears for the fate of to-morrow."[61]

THE INVASION OF MANHATTAN ISLAND

The Crown's forces began the next phase of their New York offensive on Sunday, September 15, when they came ashore at Kip's Bay. In his typically unhurried manner, William Howe had waited seventeen days before invading Manhattan Island, at least in part to allow his brother time to confer with a congressional delegation in an effort to achieve a peaceful accommodation between the opposing sides. Admiral Howe did so on September 11 at Billop Manor, the home of Loyalist Christopher Billop, on Staten Island, but his meeting with John Adams, Benjamin Franklin, and Edward Rutledge was destined to fail. The Patriot delegates would not renounce America's newly declared independence, which the Crown and Parliament insisted upon as the essential precondition to ending hostilities. According to Ambrose Serle, "it was easy to foresee what would be the Event of the Business. They met, they talked, they parted. And now nothing remains but to fight it out against a Set of the most determined Hypocrites & Demagogues, composed of the Refuse of the Colonies, that ever were permitted by Providence to be the Scourge of a Country."[62]

In his journal entry of the 15th, Serle recounted the diversionary naval maneuvers that preceded the landing of His Majesty's troops on Manhattan. These were designed to draw the defenders' attention away from the intended assault on the East River: "This Morning about 7 o'Clock, the *Renown* of 50 Guns, Capt. Banks, the *Repulse* of 32 Guns, Capt. Davis, & the *Pearl* of 32 Guns, Capt. Wilkinson, with the Schooner, Lieut. Brown, sailed up the North [Hudson] River. The morning was fine, the Tide flowed, and there was a fresh breeze. The Rebels began their Canonade as furiously as they could, but apparently with very little Effect, as their Guns were poorly served. The Ships, as these were the grand Batteries of the Enemy, returned a heavy Fire, and struck the Walls of the Batteries and the Sods of Earth, which the Rebels had raised, very frequently." The naval squadron finally anchored in the Hudson "about a Quarter before 9 . . . in view of the Fleet, at about 4 or 5 Miles Distance above it, and beyond the principal Works of the Enemy."[63]

Serle noted that while this feint played out, the final pieces of the assault were put in place: "A Transport, during the Affair upon the North River, went up the East River & joined the other Ships, almost without Molestation." The writer was quite impressed by the setting before him: "The whole Scene was awful & grand; I might say, beautiful but for the melancholy Seriousness which must attend every Circumstance, where the Lives of Men, even the basest Malefactors, are at Stake. The Hills, the Woods, the River, the Town, the Ships, and Pillars of Smoke, furnished the finest Landscape that either art and nature combined could draw, or the Imagination conceive."[64]

The Anglo-German landing at Kip's Bay followed a massive cannonade from their naval guns, beginning at ten a.m., which scattered the terrified defenders along the shoreline. The five men-of-war anchored in the East River launched their salvos at two to three hundred yards from the beach, supported by artillery on the opposite shore.[65] In Ambrose Serle's telling, "a most tremendous Discharge of Cannon from the Ships began (as was concerted) in the East River, in order to cover the Landing of the Troops upon New York Island. So terrible and so incessant a Roar of Guns few even in the Army & Navy had ever heard before. Above 70 large Pieces of Cannon were in Play, together with Swivels & small arms from the Ships, while the Batteries added to the uproar upon the Land."[66]

Any chance of serious opposition to the invasion was literally blasted by the naval firepower that terrorized the raw citizen-soldiers subjected to it. According to Joseph Plumb Martin, a sixteen-year-old private in the 5th Connecticut State Levies, one of seven state regiments that the Connecticut General Assembly created to reinforce the Continental Army in 1776, "there came such a peal of thunder from the British shipping that I thought my head would go with the sound. I made a frog's leap for the ditch, and lay as still as I possibly could, and began to consider which part of my carcass was to go first."[67]

Benjamin Trumbull, a chaplain with the Connecticut militia, detailed the unfolding scene: "A Little after Day Light on Sunday Morning Septr, 15 Two Ships of the Line and three Frigates drew

up near the Shore within Musket Shot of the Lines and entrenchments and came to Anchor there in a proper Situation to fire
most furiously upon our lines. During this Time boats were passing from [Long] Island to the Ships and men put on Board, and
about 100 Boats full of men came out of New Town Creek (Newtown in Queens County today) and made towards the Shore."
There followed Trumbull's graphic account of the assault: "The
Ships about 10 o'Clock after Firing a Signal Gun began from the
mouths of near an 100 Canon a most furious Canonade on the
Lines, which Soon levelled them almost with the Ground in some
Places, and buried our men who were in the Lines almost Sands
and Sod of Earth and made such a dust and Smoke that there was
no possibility of firing on the Enemy to any advantage, and then
not without the utmost Hazard, while the Canon poured in Such
a tremendous Fire on the Lines the Ships from their round Tops
kept up a Smart Fire with Swivels loaded with Grape Shot which
they were able to fire almost into the Entrenchments they were
so near." In the wake of this massive barrage, the king's regulars
"made good their Landing without receiving any anoyance from
our Troops. They soon marched up to the main Road and formed
across it and on the hills above our Troops in order to cut off their
Retreat. The Continental Troops now Left the Lines & there
being no General orders given how to form them that they might
Support Each other in a General Attack, or any Disposition made
for it, they attempted an escape round the Enemy in the best
manner they could, and generally made their Escape."[68]

The British anticipated, in the words of Captain Frederick
MacKenzie, that the assault would hasten "the destruction or capture of a considerable part of the rebel army." This outcome
"would be attended with numerous advantages, as it would im-
press the remainder with a dread of being surrounded and cut
off in every place where they took post, would increase their dis-
content, and probably be the means of breaking up the whole of
their army, and reducing the colonies to submission."[69]

The movement of British troops was carefully choreographed
and reflected a degree of training, experience, and precision that
could easily intimidate an adversary whose ranks were largely

filled with amateur soldiers. In addition, their attire was designed to reinforce the impression they sought to convey in battle. European armies of the time treated combat as an occasion for dressing up that required fastidious attention to the appearance they made.[70] Their uniforms sported insignia and accessories that helped to differentiate among their own regiments and between the opposing sides in the confusion of battle, but also suggested to those fighting them how formidable an enemy they were up against. The Crown's forces displayed a variety of decorations and adornments that distinguished between officers and regiments, including linings and facings of various colors, waistcoats, cockades and laces on their hats, epaulets on each shoulder, and gorgets hung around the neck.

General Howe reported to Lord George Germain, Britain's secretary of state for America and chief war strategist, that the naval maneuvers and landing on Manhattan Island proceeded like clockwork: "On the 15th inst. in the morning three ships of war passed up the North River as far as Bloomingdale, to draw the enemy's attention to that side; and the first division of troops consisting of the light infantry, the British reserve, the Hessian grenadiers and chasseurs (also known as Jägers), under the command of Lieut. Gen. Clinton . . . embarked at the head of New Town Creek, and landed about noon upon New York Island, three miles from the town, at a place called Kepp's [Kip's] Bay, under the fire of two forty gun ships and three frigates, viz. *Phoenix, Roebuck, Orpheus, Carysfort,* and *Rose.*" According to Howe, "The rebels had troops in their works round Kepp's Bay; but their attention being engaged in expectation of the King's troops landing at Stuyvesant's Cove, Horen's [Horn's] Hook, and at Harlem, which they had reason to conclude, Kepp's Bay became only a secondary object of their care. The fire of the shipping being so well directed and so incessant, the enemy could not remain in their works, and the descent was made without the least opposition."[71]

The landing occurred in two stages, the first being a four-thousand-man vanguard beginning at noon following the ferocious hour-long cannonade and encountering virtually no resistance.

Eighty-four flatboats poured forth from Newtown Creek across the East River carrying General Clinton's division, to be followed by another nine thousand troops in the afternoon. This first wave comprised the British light infantry commanded by Brigadier General Alexander Leslie, the British grenadiers led by General Cornwallis and Major General John Vaughan, and Colonel Carl von Donop's Hessian grenadiers and Jägers. Clinton had argued for a landing farther north at King's Bridge to seal off Washington's escape route to the mainland; however, doing so would have required negotiating the treacherous waters of Hell Gate and eluding the Continentals' nine-gun battery at Horn's Hook, and General Howe preferred a less risky option.[72]

The component units of Clinton's division bore distinctive traits, as each regiment in His Majesty's army contained eight companies of ordinary foot soldiers and one each of light infantry and grenadiers. The latter two occupied the regiment's flanks in battle. The light infantry companies, composed of soldiers selected from each regiment for their physical ability and fighting qualities, were primarily employed in reconnaissance and skirmishing like their American counterparts. By contrast, the grenadiers were the tallest and strongest men chosen from each regiment, and the prescribed head piece for a British grenadier— a twelve-inch-tall brimless cap—enhanced his apparent height. They were initially organized in the British army in 1678 to make use of the newly developed hand grenade by those able to throw it the farthest. (The British army had ceased to use grenades by the mid-eighteenth century, but by then the grenadiers had evolved into an elite force chosen for their size and physical condition.) Hessian grenadiers shared the same physical traits as their British counterparts, while the Jägers—an elite unit that constituted a numerically small element within the German forces in America, perhaps six hundred—functioned in a manner similar to the British light infantry and carried short, heavy, large-bore rifles without bayonets. Largely recruited from foresters and gamekeepers, they were especially adapted to fighting individually in wooded areas.[73]

General Howe anticipated more spirited opposition to Clinton's division and failed to improvise by moving inland more expeditiously when events proved otherwise. After coming ashore, the first wave of attackers waited patiently in a green meadow for reinforcements to land and their artillery to be unloaded and moved in a painfully deliberate manner. Indeed, the Crown's regulars proceeded at a cautious pace throughout this warm, sunlit day.[74]

Washington had spent the night of the 15th in a new headquarters after relocating from the Mortier mansion near the city to the upper island where various regiments were regrouping upon vacating lower Manhattan. (The mansion was built by Major Abraham Mortier, paymaster of the British army in the colony, on a twenty-six-acre estate known as Richmond Hill that was located southeast of where Varick and Charlton Streets intersect today.) He awakened at dawn in the summer home of Colonel Roger Morris, a Loyalist who had departed for England—today the Morris-Jumel Mansion at 161st Street. (Built in 1765, the mansion is the oldest house in Manhattan and is open to the public.) The view from its front portico to the south took in the village of Harlem, a small Dutch settlement ("Nieuw Haarlem") over one hundred years old with a handful of buildings, including a town hall and a church, beside the Harlem River (near today's 125th Street, just west of First Avenue).[75] Aside from enjoying this pleasant vista, the commanding general would find the day ahead a thoroughly dispiriting one.

The cannonade from British ships in the East River alerted Washington four miles away to the impending threat, and he responded promptly, as he informed John Hancock: "As soon as I heard the Firing, I road with all possible dispatch towards the place of landing when to my great surprise and Mortification I found the Troops that had been posted in the Lines retreating with the utmost precipitation and those ordered to support them, [Brigadier General Samuel P]arson's and [Brigadier General John] Fellow's Brigades flying in every direction and in the greatest confusion, notwithstanding the exertions of their Generals to form them." Washington advised the congressional president that "I used every means in my power to rally and get them into some order but my attempts were fruitless and ineffectual, and on the appearance of a small party of the Enemy, not more than Sixty or Seventy, their disorder increased and they ran away in the greatest confusion without firing a Single Shot." The distraught commander-in-chief quickly realized that any further effort to make a fighting stand with those fleeing around him was futile: "Finding that no confidence was to be placed in these Brigades and apprehending that another part of the Enemy might pass over to Harlem plains and cut off the retreat to this place, I sent orders to secure the Heights in the best manner with the Troops that were stationed on or near them, which being done, the retreat was effected with but little or no loss of Men, tho of a considerable part of our Baggage occasioned by this disgraceful and dastardly conduct."[76]

Dr. James Thacher, a Continental Army surgeon, described in his journal the chaotic response to the enemy landing: "before our army evacuated the city of New York, General Howe's army landed, under cover of five ships of war, the British and Hessians in two separate divisions. So soon as this was announced to our Commander in Chief, by a heavy cannonade from the men of war, he instantly rode toward our lines, but he was astonished and mortified to find that the troops which had been posted there, and also two brigades which had been ordered to support them, were retreating in great confusion and disorder." According to Thacher, Washington "made every effort to rally them, but without success; they were so panic struck that even the shadow of an enemy seemed to increase their precipitate flight. His Excellency, distressed and enraged, drew his sword and snapped his pistols, to check them; but they continued their flight without firing a gun; and the General, regardless of his own safety, was in so much hazard, that one of his attendants seized the reins, and gave his horse a different direction."[77]

Washington may have been as commanding a physical presence as anyone who ever commanded an army.[78] But when it came to rallying his men this day, that mattered not at all. His anguish and embarrassment at the failure to mount an effective resistance against the enemy was arguably condign punishment self-inflicted from a lack of judgment about where and how to defend Manhattan's shoreline. The commanding general had virtually neglected Kip's Bay as a possible landing site, discounting its deep water advantages to naval vessels and a spacious meadow that made for an excellent landing area. Instead, he anticipated an attack at Horn's Hook based on enemy attempts to destroy the rebel battery there and placed his best units between the village of Harlem and the battery. When British ships positioned themselves at Kip's Bay the night before the landing, Washington dispatched a force of green recruits from Colonel William Douglas's 5th Connecticut State Levies and three militia regiments to defend this site. Douglas was a capable officer—a thirty-four-year-old veteran of the French and Indian War who served under Israel Putnam in that contest, brought supplies to the American forces that invaded Canada in 1775, and raised the regiment he brought to New York—but some of his men had been with the army less than a week. The outcome was predictable.[79]

Joseph Plumb Martin of Douglas's unit recalled, "The British played their parts well; indeed, they had nothing to hinder them. We kept the lines till they [the ships' cannon] were almost levelled upon us, when our officers, seeing we could make no resistance, and no orders coming from any superior officer, and that we must soon be entirely exposed to the rake of their guns, gave the order to leave the lines. In retreating we had to cross a level clear spot of ground, forty or fifty yards wide, exposed to the whole of the enemy's fire; and they gave it to us in prime order; the grape shot and langrage flew merrily, which served to quicken our motions."[80] In point of fact, nearly all the shells flew over Douglas's men and landed in the meadow beyond, so that almost nobody was actually hit during the cannonade.[81] Nevertheless, the militia fled inland toward the Post Road, the main escape route northward, which lay not more than six hundred yards from the Kip's Bay shore. (The Post Road was the only road extending the length of Manhattan Island from New York City to King's Bridge. It ran north from the city along today's Bowery to present-day Astor Place, from where it turned slightly westward following the course of today's Broadway to Twenty-third Street. There it met the Bloomingdale Road and veered northeast while the Bloomingdale Road, the left-hand branch of the fork created by the two roads, traveled northwest. The Bloomingdale Road tracked the future path of Broadway up to today's 106th Street, from where it ran northwest until ending at a farm owned by the Hoaglandt family at present-day 115th Street and Riverside Drive. The Post Road stretched from today's Twenty-third Street and Broadway to Thirty-first Street and Lexington Avenue, then extended up the hill at Inclenberg, now Murray Hill, and turned east toward today's Turtle Bay neighborhood before turning back toward the middle of the island.) Their fear quickly spread to others, and the steadiest officers such as Colonel Douglas, who attempted to halt the panic, soon realized they had no choice but to join the retreat.[82]

The rebels' flight at Kip's Bay and the lack of organized resistance to the invasion had disastrous implications for the American troops still in New York City. By September 15, the army was in the process of moving men and equipment from lower Manhattan northward along the island's two main thoroughfares, the Post Road and the Bloomingdale Road, in order to establish a robust defensive position on Harlem Heights. That narrow rock-strewn plateau stretched for several miles across Manhattan just north of what is now 125th Street, and the line of steep bluffs on its southern side—some of them sixty feet tall—created a protective ridgeline that passed for a natural fortress. This made it a suitable rallying point for those taking flight, but over three thousand troops were still in the city when the enemy came ashore. While most of the rebels who bolted the lower island fled northward, according to Major General William Heath whose units were at King's Bridge, "some few, who could not get out of the city that way, escaped in boats over to Paulus Hook (today's Jersey City), across the river."[83] The Continentals' twenty-six-year-old artillery commander,

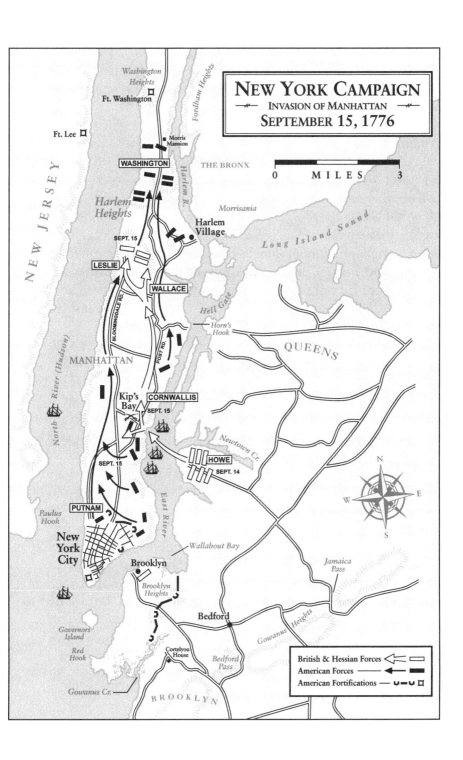

NEW YORK CAMPAIGN
—— INVASION OF MANHATTAN ——
SEPTEMBER 15, 1776

Colonel Henry Knox, seized a boat and sailed up the Hudson to join the rest of the army on the heights late that day.[84] Had General Howe's invasion occurred forty-eight hours later, there would have been no American soldiers left in lower Manhattan.[85]

When the British cannonade on the East River began, General Putnam heard it in the city. He ordered other units to reinforce the defenders wherever needed, but hardly anyone moved toward the meadow behind Kip's Bay. Many of the troops were as panicky as Douglas's men, and confusion reigned amid rumors that a retreat had been ordered. Some of the rank and file were looking for an officer to report to, even as others were running away from those commanding them. The Post Road was shortly engulfed by soldiers and horses moving in different directions but mostly heading north to the fork at Bloomingdale Road (at today's Twenty-third Street) where they turned left onto the latter instead of taking the Post Road to the right toward Kip's Bay.[86]

Putnam rode all the way from the bottom of the island to what is now Forty-second Street and Fifth Avenue, where he conferred with Washington, who was receiving reports from and issuing orders to various subordinates. Left to organize the final evacuation of Patriot troops from the city, Old Put raced back there and with his officers directed the remaining units to abandon the supplies they were attempting to secure and prepare for a forced march to Harlem Heights twelve miles away. Their column began departing at four p.m. as the second wave of Howe's troops neared completion of its landing at Kip's Bay.[87]

James Thacher detailed the movement of Putnam's force: "When retreating from New York, Major General Putnam, at the head of three thousand five hundred continental troops, was in the rear and the last that left the city. In order to avoid any of the enemy that might be advancing in the direct road to the city, he made choice of a road parallel with and contiguous to the North River, till he could arrive at a certain angle, whence another road would conduct him in such a direction as that he might form a junction with our army." The retreating Continentals were in peril because "a body of about eight thousand British and Hessians were at the same moment advancing on the road, which would have brought them in immediate contact with General Putnam, before he could have reached the turn into the other road."

The legendary intercession of a local hostess allegedly facilitated the escape of Putnam's men, or so Thacher asserted: "Most fortunately, the British generals, seeing no prospect of engaging our troops, halted their own, and repaired to the house of a Mr. Robert Murray, a quaker and friend of our cause; Mrs. Murray treated them with cake and wine, and they were induced to tarry two hours or more, Governor [William] Tryon frequently joking her about her American friends." Mrs. Murray was ostensibly instrumental in preventing the capture or destruction of the rebels in flight: "By this happy incident General Putnam, by continuing his march, escaped a rencounter with a greatly superior force, which must have proved fatal to his whole party. One half hour, it is said, would have been sufficient for the enemy to have secured the road at the turn, and entirely cut off General Putnam's retreat." Thacher reported, "It has since become almost a common saying among our officers, that Mrs. Murray saved this part of the American army."[88]

Although popular history is replete with stories of Mary Lindley Murray lavishing Madeira and cakes upon Howe and his fellow generals on a hot afternoon in order to facilitate Putnam's getaway, the legend of her heroism is, in truth, just that.[89] Notwithstanding the Murrays' vaunted reputation as hosts whose residence sat on the crest of a flat-topped hill known as Inclenberg (today's Murray Hill, just west of Lexington Avenue) and who occupied a prominent place in New York's social life, there is little reason to believe that the feminine wiles of Mary and her daughters Susannah and Beulah were deliberately employed in the Patriot cause or responsible for the salvation of Israel Putnam's column. It is doubtful she had any more knowledge of Putnam's circumstances or location than did General Howe, and the disposition of his troops at that point was not due to the Murrays' hospitality. Rather, the pre-invasion orders issued by Sir William— General Howe would be awarded the Order of the Bath for his victory at Long Island—to Henry Clinton had directed that the king's soldiers halt at Inclenberg until their entire force had come ashore, and it took some three hours—from two p.m. until almost five—for the second wave to do that.[90] Unfortunately for Howe's legacy, a known taste for women and entertainment gave rise to the notion that his self-indulgence had allowed Putnam to slip away.[91] In fact, it is more likely that he assumed the rebel troops had already vacated the lower island than that he was outwitted by an affable hostess.[92]

A more fair critique is that the British commander's caution saved the Americans from disaster because he gave the opposition more credit than was due it for being able to contest the landing.[93] Had his forces moved more aggressively to secure the roads that linked the Continentals in the city to their brethren at Harlem Heights, Howe would have trapped about one-quarter of Washington's army. Putnam's men did not begin their long march toward the upper island until well into the afternoon and only reached a point that was perpendicular to Kip's Bay perhaps six hours after the enemy had first landed. During that time, the latter failed to seal off the few avenues of escape on this narrow island that could be taken by the rebels fleeing the city.[94] Putnam's lengthy column proceeded along a route that roughly tracked the course of Eighth Avenue today and then followed the Bloomingdale Road—joining it near the present Fifty-ninth Street—up Manhattan's west side, spurred on by Old Put's animated exhortations and surprised at not encountering any of the Crown's soldiers along the way.[95] This desperate undertaking benefited greatly from the guidance provided by one of the general's aides, twenty-year-old Major Aaron Burr, who knew the area well.[96]

Once the second wave of British and Hessian troops landed at Kip's Bay, General Howe directed Generals Clinton and Cornwallis to resume their pursuit of the retreating defenders up the island. The first time all day that the Americans offered any form of organized resistance occurred when Washington called upon the Maryland Continental Regiment to act as a rear guard providing cover for the rest of the army.[97] This unit had distinguished itself at the Battle of Long Island on August 27 and in covering the army's evacuation from Brooklyn Heights two nights later, and had been posted to the Harlem section of the East River shoreline in anticipation of an enemy landing there. Its men were ordered to make an urgent stand at McGowan's Pass (around Ninety-sixth Street and Fifth Avenue near Central Park today)— seven miles north of the city—where, led by Colonel William Smallwood and Major Mordecai Gist, they dug in behind rocks and hilly terrain where the Post Road stretched between two hills before running into Harlem.[98]

Known as "Smallwood's Marylanders," this elite contingent would compile a distinguished record of service throughout the Revolutionary enterprise. It had initially been organized as a state-funded defense force supported by revenue from taxes paid by Marylanders and later the seizure of Loyalist property, and de-signed to resist a British invasion of, or Loyalist uprising within, the state. Colonel Smallwood, about forty-three, was a Maryland planter who had been educated at Eton College in England, served as an officer in the French and Indian War, and won elec-tion to the provincial assembly. Highly respected in his state, he nonetheless evinced a pettiness that did not earn him popularity with many of his soldiers.[99]

According to Smallwood, "Gen Washington expressly sent and drew our Regiment from its Brigade, to march down towards New York, to cover the Retreat and to defend the Baggage, with direc-tion to take Possession of an Advantageous Eminence near the Enemy upon the Main Road [Post Road], where we remained under Arms the best part of the Day, till Sergant's [Colonel Paul Dudley Sargent's] Brigade came in with their Baggage, who were the last Troops coming in, upon which the Enemy divided their Main Body into two Columns, one filing off on the North River endeavored to Flank and surround us, the other advancing in good order slowly up the Main Road upon us." Smallwood added that "we had orders to retreat, in good order which was done, our Corps getting within the Lines a little after Dusk."[100]

By putting up a stiff fight, the Maryland soldiers encouraged the redcoats—in this case, the light infantry brigade commanded by the able and respected General Alexander Leslie[101]—to break off and divert onto a side road called the New Bloomingdale Crossroad running west across the island to where it intersected with the Bloomingdale Road. There the British almost intercepted Putnam's column (at about today's Ninety-first Street and Broadway); however, the latter had largely passed this point when His Majesty's troops reached the Bloomingdale Road. The retreating rebels lost only one man when the last regiment in the column, the 2nd Connecticut Militia, skirmished with the invaders—Lieutenant Colonel Jabez Thompson, the regimental commander. Captain David Humphreys, who was with Putnam's exhausted force, recalled, "With no other loss we joined the army, after dark, on the heights of Harlaem. Before our brigades came in, we were given up for lost by all our friends. So critical indeed was our situation, and so narrow the gap by which we escaped, that the instant we had passed, the enemy closed it by extending their line from river to river."[102]

AT THE END OF THE DAY

When the invaders surprised Washington by landing at Kip's Bay, they had a splendid opportunity to destroy his army and perhaps finish off the rebellion by trapping a significant portion of it in the city and then overwhelming the remainder before they could organize an effective resistance or withdraw to the mainland from the island's north end. As at Long Island three weeks before, General Howe failed to deliver a crushing blow to the Patriot enterprise.

Even though Howe's troops moved just slowly enough to allow the Continentals in lower Manhattan to escape and join their comrades on the higher ground to the north, the defenders' material loss was significant. Evacuating the southern end of Manhattan so precipitately forced them to abandon a large quantity of supplies, including sixty-seven cannon—more than half the army's field pieces—and over thirteen thousand rounds of artillery ammunition.[103] Washington rued their misfortune in a letter to John Hancock: "Most of our Heavy Cannon and a part of

our Stores and provisions which we were about moving was un-
avoidably left in the City, tho every means after It had been determined in Council to evacuate the post, had been used to
prevent it."[104] According to Benjamin Trumbull, "Some Canon,
Tents, Flower and a great Deal of Baggage fell into the Enemies
Hands. This on the whole was an unfortunate Day to the American States. The loss was owing principally to a Want of Wagons &
Horses to remove the Guns and Baggage and to the Situation of
the Troops Left Behind, and the neglect in the officers, in not
forming some proper plan of Defence."[105]

The capture of New York City by Howe's army was almost ef-
fortless. A Hessian brigade swung south from Kip's Bay and moved
in along the Post Road while marines came ashore at the Grand
Battery on the city's edge. Ambrose Serle exulted in the effusive
welcome tendered by the many residents with Loyalist sympathies:
"The rebels were apparently frightened away by the horrid Din,
and deserted the Town & all their Works in the utmost Precipitation. The King's forces took possession of the Place, incredible as
it may seem, without the Loss of a Man. Nothing could equal the
Expressions of Joy, shewn by the Inhabitants, upon the arrival of
the King's officers among them. They even carried some of them
upon their shoulders about the Streets, and behaved in all re-
spects, Women as well as Men, like overjoyed Bedlamites."[106] More
than seven hundred people would sign a "declaration of dependence" avowing their loyalty to Great Britain.[107]

The rebel army had again tasted bitter defeat. About sixty of
its men were dead or wounded with three hundred captured, and
many of those who escaped the enemy advance and reached the
safety of Harlem Heights were both fatigued and traumatized by
the day's events. The only conspicuous talent the Continentals
demonstrated in their immediate response to the Kip's Bay landing was the one they had exhibited on August 27—running
away.[108] Philip Vickers Fithian, a Presbyterian minister who had
been appointed chaplain to the New Jersey militia serving with
the Continental Army, lamented this state of affairs in his journal
on the night of September 15: "Just Heaven thy Judgments are

equal—We are a sinful Nation, O Lord. But is it written in thy Book concerning us that we must always fly before our Enemies?"[109] For the rest of the war, George Washington set his sights on recapturing New York City.[110] However, it would take seven grueling years and a final peace treaty with Great Britain for him to ride triumphantly down the Post Road and make his grand entrance.

TWO

The Rise of
Thomas Knowlton

IN HIS CLASSIC WORK on the Battle of Harlem Heights from 1897, historian Henry P. Johnston makes pointed reference to the fact that Lieutenant Colonel Thomas Knowlton and the men he led in his ranger unit on September 16, 1776, precipitated and were especially prominent in that engagement.[1] They were part of an elite force, known as Knowlton's Rangers, which George Washington—out of a desperate need for information about the enemy and his respect for Knowlton's competence and daring—had asked him to command and tasked with conducting dangerous covert operations.[2] With the possible exception of his role at the Battle of Bunker Hill, this was the colonel's defining moment in combat. It would also be his last. The perception of Knowlton as one of the best regimental commanders in the Continental Army,[3] as a colonel with the reputation of a general,[4] as a fearless officer who led his adoring soldiers by example,[5] and as someone whose death cut off a man otherwise destined to be a great general,[6] reinforces one's sense of the enormity of loss at Harlem Plains to what Washington termed "the "glorious Cause"[7] of American independence.

References to Knowlton's life and military career appear among a miscellany of primary and secondary sources, but as yet no single work has captured his story.[8] The fullest biographical sketch comes to us from Dr. Ashbel Woodward (1804–1885) in his *Memoir of Col. Thomas Knowlton, of Ashford, Connecticut*, published in the New England Historical and Genealogical Register in January 1861. The physician-author, who like his subject lived in Ashford as a boy,[9] began his chronicle by expressing disappointment at the lack of recognition given the Patriot stalwart, observing that "not a few brave men who sacrificed fortune and life to secure our national independence—men held in high esteem by the most honored of their contemporaries—have been allowed a very inadequate place in the national records and the national remembrance." Woodward was resolute in his conviction that as to the Connecticut colonel, "the position has not been awarded to him in the history of the colonial and revolutionary periods, to which his sagacity and valor, his patriotism and distinguished public service entitle him."[10]

The testimony of Knowlton's peers conveys the image and substance of someone admired by virtually all who knew him, an exceedingly able figure who excelled as both a farmer and an officer, and who believed in leading from the front, seemingly oblivious to the attendant danger. One of the soldiers in his command, Sergeant David Thorp of Woodbury, Connecticut, recounted, "He did not say 'go boys,' but 'come boys,' and we always were ready and willing to follow him."[11]

AN IMAGE FOR POSTERITY

Thomas Knowlton occupies a conspicuous place in John Trumbull's painting from 1786, *The Death of General Warren at the Battle of Bunker's Hill, June 17, 1775*, which presents a collective portrait of the more prominent actors in that storied engagement and ranks among the most famous works of art in American history.

A Harvard College graduate familiar with the Boston area, Trumbull was serving with a Connecticut regiment and stationed in nearby Roxboro in June 1775. He witnessed firsthand the destruction that accompanied the first major engagement of the war at Bunker Hill—actually Breed's Hill, according to most historians.[12] The young soldier heard the cannon blasts from the Royal Navy's warships directed against Charlestown, which preceded the British infantry attack against the rebel positions on and about the hill just north of Boston, and saw through his field glasses fires breaking out "among the buildings of the town, which soon extended rapidly, and enveloped the whole in flames."[13]

As Trumbull saw it, the Revolution was a monumental struggle between good and evil.[14] In 1785, he began mapping out the paintings that would embody his plan to commemorate that struggle by visually recreating the great events of the war. The artist began the first painting, his image of the Bunker Hill battle, in the fall of 1785 and finished it early the next year. Ironically, Trumbull gave birth to his masterpiece in London, where he had been studying and practicing his craft since 1784.

Abigail Adams viewed the picture for the first time while visiting Britain's metropolis—her husband John was posted as America's first ambassador there—and reported her impressions to Elizabeth Smith Shaw: "It is the work of one of our own Countrymen, and of one of the most important events of the late War. Mr Trumble has made a painting of the battle at Char[le]stown and the Death of Generall Warren. To speak of its merit, I can only say; that in looking at it, my whole frame contracted, my Blood Shiverd and I felt a faintness at my Heart." Abigail, who would convey her impressions of Trumbull's handiwork to her husband, further observed: "He is the first painter who has undertaking to immortalize by his Pencil those great actions; that gave Birth to our Nation. By this means he will not only secure his own fame, but transmit to Posterity Characters and actions which will command the admiration of future ages and prevent the period which gave birth to them from ever passing away into the dark abiss of time whilst he teaches, mankind, that it is not rank, or titles, but Character alone which interest Posterity."[15]

Trumbull created a guide to his painting that identifies seventeen figures.[16] Being unable to compose life portraits of them all, he had to rely on the work of other artists or in some cases make up his own visual impression.[17] Dr. Joseph Warren lies mortally wounded in the foreground just to the left of center, cradled by an unknown militiaman in bare feet seeking to avert a grenadier's bayonet with his left arm, and with Thomas Knowlton standing over them. In actuality, Warren was killed instantly as the Americans fled their redoubt on Breed's Hill, shot in the back of the head.[18]

Warren's central presence in the painting, and the use of his name in its title, reflected his status as a popular hero and a pre-eminent advocate for colonial rights, although he was neither a militiaman nor a real officer and as such was never expected to fight in the battle. His designation as a major-general by the Massachusetts Provincial Congress, over which Warren presided, three days before the British attack owed itself to his Revolutionary leadership as a civilian and respect for his stature as the foremost physician in the Boston community.[19] But his position in the picture, adjacent to the barefooted militiaman and Knowlton—with all three among the most clearly visible in the furious aggregation of combatants—begs the question whether there was an implied connection between them.

Trumbull depicts Knowlton wearing a white shirt with a tan vest and holding a musket by his waist pointed at the British, his firearm in that position presumably to reflect the lack of ammunition that prevented the Americans from fending off the final enemy charge. His facial expression is one of grim determination, and his bearing suggests a defiant presence that can only be removed by a fatal blow—true to life in that respect but not until the Battle of Harlem Heights. One wonders whether his white shirt is symbolic of what Trumbull regarded as the purity of the Patriot cause generally or the noble character of a citizen-soldier defending hearth and home, or both. Knowlton was then a captain with the 5th Company of the 3rd Connecticut Regiment under General Israel Putnam, who appears at the far left of the painting. Behind Knowlton is Colonel William Prescott, the officer who commanded those defending the redoubt at Breed's Hill, wearing a wide-brim hat.

More than a century after Trumbull unveiled Knowlton's visage, a descendant of his favorably assessed the authenticity of the image. Judge Samuel Utley of Worcester, Massachusetts, a great-grandson of Knowlton and a charter member of the Knowlton Association of America formed in 1895 by family members and close associates, observed that the artist must have known his subject well: "Many members of the family bear striking resemblance to the picture and we think it safe to call it a likeness of him."[20]

John Trumbull clearly revealed the extent of his regard for Knowlton by assigning him a prominent position in the foreground of this scene, even placing him in front of Colonel Prescott.[21] Furthermore, his image of the man is doubly enshrined for posterity, as it is the sole authority for Knowlton's likeness in a bronze statue that has been standing on the grounds of the Connecticut State Capitol in Hartford since 1895.[22] It is unknown whether the artist's estimation of his fellow Connecticuter was influenced to any extent by their shared geographic identity; however, Knowlton earned his place in the painting with a performance on June 17, 1775, that made him something of a legend among his comrades-in-arms and offered a foretaste of the exemplary standard for combat leadership that he would embody in George Washington's army.[23]

EARLY LIFE

Thomas Knowlton's forebears arrived in New England by boat long before he arrived by birth. His family of English origin ranked among the earliest settlers in the Massachusetts Bay Colony, with an ancestor, John Knowlton—the eldest of three brothers—reported to be in Ipswich as early as 1639. John's younger brothers, William and Deacon Thomas, also settled there. They were the sons of Captain William Knowlton and along with their widowed mother emigrated from England in about 1632.

In 1728, John's great-grandson William, a farmer and skilled carpenter known as a "housewright,"[24] married Martha Pinder of Boxford in Essex County just north of Boston. Her great-grand-father Henry Pynder had relocated from England in 1635. Their third son, Thomas, the seventh of nine children, was born in West Boxford on November 22, 1740.[25] He was preceded by Mary, Sarah, William, Lucy who died young, a second daughter named Lucy, and Daniel, and followed by Priscilla and Nathaniel.

In 1748, the family moved to Ashford in northeastern Connecti-cut, a village in Windham County cleaved by the Mount Hope River. It was founded in 1714 and named after the large number of ash trees growing in the neighboring forests. The county had been formally organized in 1726 and, aside from Ashford, con-tained seven other towns: Canterbury, Killingly, Plainfield, Pom-fret, Voluntown, Windham, and Woodstock. It is bordered on the north by Worcester County in Massachusetts, on the east by Prov-idence and Kent Counties in Rhode Island, on the south by New London County, and on the west by Tolland County.

The farm that William purchased in the western part of Ash-ford, near the village church, spread over four hundred acres nes-tled among the picturesque rolling hills of what would later become known as the "Quiet Corner."[26] His holding was consid-erably larger than the average amount of land owned by a Con-necticut family—166 acres in 1750. The terrain embraced part of the hilly uplands of Windham County known for its thin soil, and in this hilly, rocky region, farmers specialized in cattle as the qual-ity of land dictated its use for beef and dairy production.[27]

William died on March 13, 1753, at age forty-eight, and his land would be divided among his sons. According to a late nine-teenth-century account of the history of Ashford, Thomas and his second-oldest brother, Daniel (born in December 1738), who saw action together in two wars, became diligent farmers. After "serv-ing brilliantly" while fighting against the French and Indians in the 1750s, they "engaged with equal ardor in cultivating their land and discharging the ordinary civil and military duties of good citizens."[28]

The Knowltons enjoyed a relative degree of prosperity that supported their family and bolstered their social standing in the community. Farm life was central to the daily existence of colonial America, but it offered its practitioners a wearying routine. An early nineteenth-century biography of Israel Putnam, another Windham County farmer who would serve with Thomas Knowlton in two wars and become a general in the second, spoke of the "stubborn and patient industry" required of a farmer in that time and place, which included, in addition to building and maintaining a house and barn, "making fences, sowing grain, planting orchards, and taking care of his stock," as well as coping with the challenges posed by summer droughts, searing heat during the fall harvest, the loss of cattle in winter, and the threat to sheep from predatory creatures.[29]

Thomas Knowlton's formal education, like that of the vast majority of colonial youth, was limited to the narrow course of study typifying instruction in the common schools of the time. The latter emphasized reading but also taught writing and arithmetic within their respective purviews.[30] Learning occurred at home, in church, and in the local schoolhouse, but in terms of classroom-based instruction, Knowlton's experience was probably similar to that of George Washington, eight years Knowlton's senior, who in his Virginia youth had little formal schooling and so was deprived of the liberal education for which gentlemen were noted and of which several of the most celebrated Founding Fathers could boast—among them John Adams, Thomas Jefferson, Alexander Hamilton, and James Madison. Like Washington, Knowlton received the equivalent of a grade-school education in a country classroom, which conspicuously lacked the instruction in Latin, Greek, and French that a university experience afforded and that marked a truly learned person.

Both Washington and Knowlton lost their fathers early, the former when he was eleven and the latter at age twelve, which would have required them to shoulder a load of responsibilities that foreclosed any opportunity for extensive schooling. Yet both men were highly intelligent. Ashbel Woodward, Knowlton's nineteenth-century biographer, recalled from his boyhood in Ashford the impressions of the town's elders who knew Knowlton and conveyed a sense of his naturally bright intellect that, when combined with his ability to learn from the experiences and associations of military life, "caused his companionship to be sought by the most cultivated."[31]

By the time he reached adolescence, Thomas Knowlton stood at least six feet tall, well above average for his time. His complexion was light and his hair dark. Woodward described him, in the hagiographic tones of a nineteenth-century chronicler, as being "erect and elegant in figure, and formed more for activity than strength" with "eyes of deep spiritual beauty."[32] Even a twenty-first-century work of history speaks no less admiringly of his appearance: "as tall as Washington . . . muscular and trim, sporting the square jawline of a superhero and the boyish good looks of a prince."[33] That said, the Connecticut youth needed more than prepossessing physical attributes to survive the challenge that lay ahead of him. He has been called courageous to a fault.[34] And in this he was also like Washington. The hallmarks of Knowlton's leadership—competence, daring, fortitude, and practical intelligence—would first be displayed as a teenaged wilderness warrior.

A YOUNG SOLDIER

Young Knowlton became embroiled in the global struggle between Britain and France from 1756 to 1763, known as the Seven Years' War in Europe and the French and Indian War in America, which established the British empire as the most formidable on earth in the final and most decisive of America's colonial wars.[35] The defeat of General Edward Braddock, commander-in-chief of the Crown's forces in North America, and his army of British troops, provincial soldiers, and colonial militia at the Monongahela River in July 1755 rendered several American colonies, including Connecticut, vulnerable to incursions by marauding French and Indian war parties in the early years of the conflict.

Connecticut's General Assembly responded by putting at least 2,500 men under arms in the first year and by the end of hostilities had raised more than thirty thousand men by enlistments, detachments from existing organizations, and impressment. This figure far exceeded that of any other colony involved in the war effort as a percentage of its population.[36] An estimated 60 percent of Connecticut men in their prime military age served in the provincial ranks.[37]

The enlistment of Connecticut's troops throughout the war was generally authorized for a single campaign at a time. The General Assembly voted in February or March of each year to raise a stipulated number of men, from which ensued the recruiting and equipping of a new provincial force for the coming campaign to operate in conjunction with British regular units. The enlistees began their service in the spring and were mustered out in the fall. Thomas Knowlton and his older brother Daniel served together through most of the conflict, attending to their farmstead responsibilities during the winter months and then joining the ranks by May 1 each year. Along the way, they became experienced soldiers and Thomas gained recognition for his leadership abilities.

Daniel first enlisted in 1756 at the age of seventeen and his younger brother at age sixteen the following year. In 1757, Thomas joined the 8th Company of the only Connecticut regiment raised that year, serving as a private under Captain John Slapp, but also spent time in a militia company led by Captain Daniel Cone. He was listed at a muster call of the north military company of East Haddam, Connecticut, on August 9, 1757.

In 1758, Private Knowlton was assigned to the 10th Company of the 3rd Connecticut Regiment under Captain Jedediah Fay. He gained valuable military experience serving in the same regiment as Major Israel Putnam and Lieutenant Robert Durkee, who had both seen action with Rogers's Rangers—the colonials commanded by Captain, and soon to be Major, Robert Rogers. They were assigned tasks no other units could or would carry out.

As in earlier colonial wars in North America, the provincial regiments supporting British forces included ranger companies that served as a substitute for the Indian allies whom Britain lacked. The rangers often acted as scouts and guides between British outposts and conducted reconnaissance missions to ascertain the location and condition of French units, as well as launching raids into hostile territory to disrupt enemy operations where feasible and taking stragglers as prisoners. These ventures entailed long marches through heavily wooded terrain that were attended by uncertainty regarding the location of their foe, and the other hardships and dangers of wilderness warfare. All of this required certain distinctive attributes on the part of the officers leading these woodland expeditions and the young men who followed them: physical stamina, courage, boldness, and keen wits. Thomas Knowlton made full use of these while fighting alongside Rogers's irregular soldiers. Over time, the colonial rangers became the subject of military legend and popular fascination.[38] Ranger companies were first employed in this war—during the expedition against the French fort at Crown Point on Lake Champlain—in the form of a New Hampshire company under Captain Rogers and Lieutenant John Stark, and their number grew rapidly: to three in 1756, four in 1757, and nine in 1758.

Rogers may have authored the first written manual of warfare in America.[39] He set forth twenty-eight rules to serve as standing orders for his Rangers, prescribing equipment and tactics, which would inform the operational mindset of men like Thomas Knowlton and Israel Putnam in this and the next war. They were to proceed single-file when in the field and operating in small numbers, "keeping at such a distance from each other as to prevent one shot from killing two men." When pursuing the retreating enemy, the Rangers were directed to send out flanking parties and prevent their foe "from gaining eminences, or rising grounds." If they were forced to retreat, Rogers instructed his men to "let the front of your whole party fire and fall back, till the rear hath done the same, making for the best ground you can" and subjecting the enemy to constant fire. He ordered the Rangers, in the face of an enemy advance, to "reserve your fire till they approach very near, which will then put them into the greater surprise and consternation, and give you an opportunity of rushing upon them with your hatchets and cutlasses to the better advantage."[40]

Private Knowlton first distinguished himself in combat during the Battle of Wood Creek in August 1758. A force commanded by Major Rogers, comprising his Rangers and other colonials along with British soldiers, was attacked while advancing through the woods by a similar number of French and Indians near Wood Creek, a critical waterway for moving forces and supplies from Fort Stanwix to Oneida Lake and on to British units near Lake Ontario. (Wood Creek is a river in central New York State that runs westward from the city of Rome to Oneida Lake. Its waters flow ultimately to Lake Ontario, the easternmost of the five Great Lakes.) According to Rogers, his column sortied from Fort Anne—about ten miles east of the southern part of Lake George—early on the morning of August 8: "Major Putnam with a party of Provincials marching in the front, my Rangers in the rear, Capt. [James] Dalyell with the [British] regulars in the center, the other officers suitably disposed among the men, being in number 530, exclusive of officers (a number having by leave returned home the day before). After marching about three-quarters of a mile, a fire began with five hundred of the enemy in front; I brought my people into as good order as possible."[41]

Israel Putnam was with the 3rd Company of the 3rd Connecticut Regiment, while Private Knowlton—with the 10th Company of the same regiment—had been detached from Rogers's main force as part of a scouting party supporting Captain John Durkee's 9th company. Their mission was to intercept French and Indian stragglers thought to be roaming the forested terrain in the vicinity of Wood Creek, at the same time as the main body under Rogers and Putnam combed the woodland east of Lake George. While probing the area, Knowlton's party took possession of a recently occupied encampment; there they found kettles and other objects indicating the occupants' intention to return and prepared to engage them. A day or two passed without any action, at which point French boats that were spotted on the creek detected the presence of the provincial soldiers. With their location known, Knowlton and the others abandoned the encampment and warily advanced single-file into a thick forest searching for the enemy, who greeted them with a hail of bullets from the dense undergrowth. As the colonials could discern their adversary's position only from the sound of musket fire and the smoke from gun barrels, they took cover behind any available tree and returned fire.

Knowlton and the others in his party were largely forced to fight independently of each other in these confused and frantic moments. A quivering in the brush and the movement of an Indian crawling from the undergrowth into a path just created by the provincials' footsteps caught Knowlton's eye. He immediately shot and killed the Indian, reloaded his firearm, and then leaped forth to secure the dead man's scalp as a trophy—a practice common among both colonials and Indians.[42] However, as Knowlton reached the body, he was surrounded by ten or twelve Indians who suddenly sprang from the grass. They did not fire, perhaps in fear of hitting each other, but rather each beckoned the youth to surrender to him. Without hesitation, Knowlton shot the nearest warrior, sprang over his prostrate body, and lunged into the thicket. His would-be captors, momentarily stunned by his audacity and agility, paused just long enough to allow him to make his escape through a shower of musket balls as the fleet-footed adolescent dashed off in the direction of his fellow provincials.

By now a general action had ensued. The Battle of Wood Creek was on, and the two sides were embroiled in an intense and confused struggle marked by fierce individual encounters between combatants fighting desperately for survival. At one point, Knowlton and a burly French soldier spied each other as they entered a small clearing from the opposite side; each took aim at the other but their muskets misfired. Neither man had a bayonet. Thomas rushed his adversary who was drawing a dagger, grabbed him by the waist and tried to throw him to the ground, but his larger and stronger foe threw him instead. Fortunately for the overmatched stripling, another American entered the clearing at that moment and the outnumbered Frenchman surrendered. Once Knowlton had reprimed his musket, the two provincials headed for the rear with their prisoner, when he suddenly broke away in an ill-considered attempt at escape—only to be thwarted by a fatal shot from Knowlton.

Being separated from the main body of troops, Knowlton and his companion were forced to make their way back to their lines alone and through enemy fire. They ran in various directions until reaching safety, and Knowlton escaped injury despite sustaining a bullet hole in the shoulder of his coat. For his actions that day, the enterprising seventeen-year-old received the first of his promotions—to sergeant.[43]

Having survived his ordeal at Wood Creek, Thomas Knowlton's 1758 campaign ended when he was discharged on November 20 and returned to Ashford. There he found time during intervals between his wartime service to become a husband and father. He courted Anna Keyes, daughter of Sampson Keyes of Ashford. Thomas was eighteen and Anna fifteen when they married on April 5, 1759; and Frederick, the first of their nine children—two of whom died in infancy—would arrive eighteen months later. The adolescent newlyweds had little time to enjoy connubial life before the start of that year's military campaign summoned the new husband to duty as sergeant in the 3rd Company of the 1st Connecticut Regiment, again serving under John Slapp, who had become a major.

In July 1759, Knowlton and his regiment participated in an expedition led by General Jeffrey Amherst, commander-in-chief of the British army in North America, against Fort Ticonderoga (named "Fort Carillon" by the French) at the head of Lake Champlain in northeastern New York. Amherst's ten-thousand-man force comprised seven regiments of regulars and nine of New England colonials in addition to nine ranger companies. One year after a previous such undertaking had ended in humiliating failure, the Anglo-American troops found the fort held by only a token garrison, and it fell in four days at a cost to them of only five dead and thirty-one wounded. The capture of Fort Ticonderoga did not end Sergeant Knowlton's 1759 campaign, however, as he was included in a muster roll of his company there on October 18 and returned to Ashford and Anna for the winter once his duty ended.

Amherst's capture of the last French stronghold, Montreal, on September 9, 1760, effectively ended the war in North America, and Knowlton saw the enemy flag furled there.[44] He had become a commissioned officer at the beginning of that year's campaign with a promotion to ensign while still serving in the 3rd Company of the 1st Connecticut Regiment under Major Slapp. (An ensign carried an infantry company's colors and was its lowest commissioned officer, ranking below the captain and lieutenant.) The offensive against Montreal—the principal objective of the 1760 campaign—was undertaken by a combined force of three British armies and provincial units from Connecticut, New Jersey, and New York. Among them was Israel Putnam, now a lieutenant colonel commanding the 2nd Company of the 4th Connecticut Regiment.

Once the fighting ended for the winter, Knowlton returned to the farm where his first child, Frederick, was born on December 4. The new father resumed his military pursuits on April 1, 1761, as ensign with the 10th Company of the 1st Connecticut Regiment under Captain Robert Durkee and was discharged on December 3. His brother Daniel, who had served in the same unit as Thomas in prior years, did so again as a sergeant in the 10th Company.

In 1762, Knowlton received another promotion—to second lieutenant in the same company, now under Captain Hugh Ledlie. He was all of twenty-one and boasted a growing reputation as someone well equipped to handle the challenges of combat and command. Lieutenant Knowlton's new assignment in the 10th Company began on March 15, two days before Daniel's.

Hostilities in Canada were largely concluded, but the conflict took a new turn with Great Britain's declaration of war against Spain, France's putative ally, on January 4, 1762, and Madrid's response in kind fourteen days later. The theater of operations in the Western Hemisphere expanded to include the Spanish dominion of Cuba, as British forces in America received orders to launch an expedition against Havana. The island's capital of thirty-five thousand was the largest city in the West Indies and the most heavily fortified port in the Americas.

The expedition under George Keppel, earl of Albemarle, sailed from England on March 6 and reached the West Indies by April 20. Albemarle quickly isolated the Havana garrison and laid siege to the city, but he soon encountered a more formidable opponent than the defenders: a combination of tropical disease, oppressive heat, and insufficient potable water that would kill or wound several thousand men. Even so, the arrival of additional troops from North America—half regulars and half provincials—proved enough to overcome the Havana garrison. Its surrender on August 14 ended a campaign that imposed a staggering toll on British regulars and provincials, with the overwhelming majority of losses due to disease. (Britain's control of Cuba lasted only six months. Havana would be returned to Spain by the Treaty of Paris in 1763 as part of a global exchange of territory that included Spain's surrender of Florida to Britain.)

Of the 2,300 colonial troops who landed in Cuba in mid-summer after sailing from the Port of New York, about one thousand were from Connecticut. The latter comprised the 1st Connecticut Regiment, which included the Knowlton brothers in the 10th Company. Israel Putnam, as lieutenant colonel of the regiment, assumed immediate command of the Connecticut troops, while General Phineas Lyman of Suffield was appointed overall commander of the provincial units. Almost 60 percent of the Connecticut Regiment died before their return home.[45] Six ships carried the remaining Connecticut soldiers from Havana back to the Port of New York in October, although many of the ill did not make it back alive.

Lieutenant Knowlton had survived the hellish campaign but faced yet another peril during the return voyage. He was challenged to a duel by a British officer whom Knowlton had reproached as being the worse for drink. The incident ended uneventfully, however, when further reflection cooled the Englishman's ardor. He withdrew his challenge before their ship reached land and offered an apology, having either admitted his wrongdoing or calculated the risks of going through with the affair.[46]

BETWEEN THE WARS

Thomas Knowlton's war came to an end with his discharge on December 10, 1762, following his brother Daniel by six days. After six years of military service and four major campaigns that included the capture of Fort Ticonderoga and Montreal and near-death experiences at the Battle of Wood Creek and the siege of Havana (one from combat, the other from disease), the twenty-two-year-old was a virtuoso in the grim realities of armed combat with a corresponding maturity that made him old beyond his years. He had earned three promotions, rising from private to lieutenant in less than four years, and in the process received a rigorous and extended education in the art of war and the value and practice of reconnaissance, tactical mobility, adroit maneuvering, and battlefield cunning. Now the more prosaic existence of a Windham County farmer awaited him, along with Anna and two-year-old Frederick.

Family and farm dominated the years between two wars for Knowlton, as it did for many a veteran of the recent conflict. While he toiled on his rocky Windham County acreage, the number of mouths for him and Anna to feed steadily multiplied. After Frederick's birth in late 1760, there followed eight others in rapid succession: Sally on November 23, 1763; Thomas on July 13, 1765; Polly on January 11, 1767; Abigail on June 20, 1768; Sampson on February 8, 1770—who lived for only seven months; Anna on June 8, 1771—who lived for only a year; a second daughter named Anna on May 19, 1773; and Lucinda on November 10, 1776. The latter would be born almost two months after her father's death. Still, domestic obligations did not deter the clan's young patriarch from engaging in public affairs both in Ashford and the wider community.

One indication of Knowlton's public standing is his selection as a member of a sheriff's jury or committee from Windham County that was impaneled to determine the route of a new highway and whether any landholders would be compensated for resulting damages. The jury's decision of March 18, 1769, was signed by several people, including at the very end "Thos. Knolton"—

evidence that his surname was later changed to add a "w."[47] In addition to that, the document is noteworthy because of how rare it is to find Knowlton's signature.[48]

Further evidence of Knowlton's public stature lies in his being chosen as a member of the board of selectmen in Ashford in 1773. For someone only thirty-two years of age to serve on the local governing body reflected a widespread recognition of his prominence in the community and the qualities that had stood him in good stead throughout the last war—a quick mind, astute judgment, the courage of his convictions, and the respect of others. Knowlton had clearly established himself as one of the foremost citizens in Ashford. That, plus his record as a war veteran, would enhance his visibility as someone to whom others in the village looked for leadership when the storm clouds of Anglo-American friction gathered in the early 1770s and the increasingly strained relations between Britain and its North American dominions presaged an armed struggle over the latter's right of political and economic self-determination.

Knowlton and his community could not help but be impacted by the revolutionary spirit spreading throughout the land and no less so than in their corner of Connecticut, with Windham County bordering on the colony where tensions first came to a head. Further south in New Haven, young James Hillhouse reflected the public mood among restive Connecticut Patriots when he wrote his fellow Yale graduate Nathan Hale, schoolmaster at the Union School in New London, in July 1774 to urge his involvement in the approaching trial by fire: "Liberty is our reigning Topic, which loudly calls upon every one to Exert his Tallants & abilities to the utmost in defending of it—now is the time for heroes—now is the time for great men to immortalize their names in the deliverance of their Country, and grace the annals of America with their Glorious deeds."[49]

The colonial-policy initiatives adopted in London soon after the French and Indian War ended set off a chain of events in which many, if not most, Americans sought to resist what they perceived as provocative actions by Parliament that encroached on their autonomy, and the latter responded by asserting its imperial sovereignty over these recalcitrant subjects. Hopes for an amicable settlement of their differences gradually yielded to a widespread sense that bloodshed was unavoidable. That expectation met reality on April 19, 1775, when 1,500 of His Majesty's regulars—dispatched from Boston into the Massachusetts countryside in search of rebel arms—traded fire with local militia at Lexington and Concord and on their way back to the city. For General Thomas Gage, commander of the British troops in North America and military governor of Massachusetts, the results of this expedition were ominous: a casualty rate of almost 20 percent among the redcoats and an outpouring of musket-toting civilians who gathered in Cambridge and sealed off Boston from the interior. A siege that would last nearly eleven months had begun.

THE APPROACHING STORM

Among Thomas Knowlton's neighbors in Ashford and throughout Windham County, Patriot fever rose from 1765 onward as they learned of developments just to their north. Local committees of correspondence had been appointed in reaction to the news of various parliamentary decrees in order to maintain communication among the towns in Windham and with those in neighboring counties. Many elected to boycott imported British luxuries, including food, drink, and dress, while Ashford and her sister towns held meetings where seditious sentiments were expressed and actions taken to reflect the public mood. In particular, the closing of the Port of Boston by Parliament in 1774 and the appeal by its Patriot leaders to the various colonies for food and other supplies prompted the communities in Windham to respond with expressions of support for Boston's economically hard-pressed citizens. Town meetings voted to pass resolutions of sympathy and make substantial contributions for their relief, which included flocks of sheep from farms throughout the county that were driven north along with other animals.

Knowlton's fellow war veteran and Windham farmer Israel Putnam, appointed lieutenant colonel of Connecticut's militia regiment that year, personally delivered 125 sheep on a ninety-mile journey from his Pomfret farmstead to Boston. There he was greeted by its leading citizens and welcomed as a houseguest by Dr. Joseph Warren, befitting Putnam's status as the most famous resident of eastern Connecticut based on his military exploits against the French and Indians.[50] His active support for Boston's resistance to London's edicts undoubtedly influenced others in Windham County and beyond, especially former comrades-in-arms such as Knowlton.

A convention of delegates from New London and Windham counties, held at Norwich on September 9, 1774, urged each of their towns to supply itself with a full complement of ammunition and military stores. The delegates further resolved that the various militia companies equip themselves at once and take steps to prepare for action, including training those unfamiliar with handling arms and military routine, and ensuring proper instruction in the relevant skills and discipline. In October, the Connecticut General Assembly directed each town in the colony to double its available quantity of powder, musket balls, and flints. The few Loyalists about took care not to exhibit their sentiments too openly in the face of growing support among their neighbors for resisting Britain's insistence on parliamentary sovereignty.[51]

JOINING UP

In the spring of 1775, Thomas Knowlton, now a seasoned thirty-four years of age, was managing the roles of husband, farmer, father of six, Ashford selectman, and member of his town's militia company. As it did for others, the delicate balance between such obligations was upset on April 20 when news came to Ashford of the fighting at Lexington and Concord. Israel Putnam, for one, was plowing that morning when he heard what had happened and left his son to unyoke the team while he hurried off to consult with others in the community and especially militia officers before riding to Cambridge. When Putnam learned the British had retreated to Boston, he returned to Connecticut but then raised a regiment and led it on to Cambridge. Meanwhile, armed citizens began to gather in the several Windham County towns, and not a few men gathered up their muskets and powder and started for Boston without waiting for any organized response from the militia units.

Fifteen companies gathered at Pomfret, the agreed-upon rendezvous for volunteers from the county. Knowlton, who had joined the Ashford Company as a private, was unanimously chosen captain by a vote of its seventy-eight members. A council of officers from the various companies determined that one-fifth of the men present should depart for Cambridge immediately and the remainder return to their homes for the time being. The entire Ashford Company, as well as a large number of men from Pomfret and a few selected from other companies present, were chosen to march at once. They were under the command of Lieutenant Colonel Experience Storrs, but he only accompanied these militia as far as Dudley, where he left them under the command of Captain Knowlton and another officer. Upon reaching Cambridge, they became the first contingent of trained volunteers to arrive from beyond Massachusetts and thereby conferred that distinction upon Windham County, while Knowlton's Ashford men became the first full militia company from outside the colony to appear there. Other companies were soon called for and rapidly appeared outside Boston, including those from various towns in Windham.

Knowlton left his wife with a large brood to care for and a farm to manage when he headed to Cambridge. To add to Anna's burden, he took with him their oldest son, Frederick, who would otherwise have helped considerably to alleviate her stress and strain. Obviously it was common for a soldier to leave a family behind when he joined up with the regular army or his militia unit, but not all took along a boy as young as fourteen—although some surely did.

Anna may have let it be known that she wanted her husband to stay at home to care for his family and tend to his responsibilities as a governing official in Ashford.[52] In any case, she was forced to confront the challenges faced by women on the home front—the devastating sense of loneliness after her husband and son departed, the care of young children, shortages of everyday necessities such as pins and medicines, spiraling prices that made it difficult to purchase goods even if they were available, and the absence of family members who in this case normally tilled the fields. She would have had to ensure that the daily tasks associated with life on a farmstead were performed as needed, such as mending fences, cutting and storing firewood, and repairing tools, and that routine domestic chores were as well, whether it was feeding a baby, watching children, cooking meals, weeding gardens, or sewing clothes.[53]

Patriot sentiment was on display throughout Connecticut in response to the news from Massachusetts. Chief among those venting was Governor Trumbull, upon whom Washington would bestow the sobriquet "Brother Jonathan."[54] From Hartford, he warned General Gage that the people of his colony "beg leave to assure your Excellency, that as they apprehend themselves justified by the principles of self-defence, so they are most *firmly* resolved to defend their rights and privileges to the last extremity; nor will they be restrained from giving aid to their brethren, if any unjustifiable attack is made upon them."[55]

On April 26, 1775, the Connecticut General Assembly appointed three general officers of the colony's militia, including Israel Putnam as second brigadier general. He was also made colonel of the 3rd Regiment and captain of its 1st Company. The legislators voted to raise six thousand men by calling out a quarter of the militia—to be divided into six regiments, each with ten companies of one hundred men—and in May they began marching to Boston. The Ashford Company became the 5th Company of the 3rd Connecticut Regiment, with Putnam as regimental colonel. Except for Putnam, the company officers were from Ashford: Thomas Knowlton, captain; Reuben Marcy, first lieutenant; John Keyes, second lieutenant; and Daniel Allen, Jr., ensign. The 3rd Regiment's ten companies included men from New London and Windham counties.

BUNKER HILL

Every day, militiamen from Connecticut, Maine (then part of Massachusetts), New Hampshire, and Rhode Island arrived in Cambridge to join those from Massachusetts. At General Putnam's initiative, the citizen-soldiers from Massachusetts and Connecticut began constructing fortifications, and on May 13 he led over two thousand men from Cambridge onto the Charlestown Peninsula in a blatant act of defiance against the Crown's troops across the Charles River in Boston. They returned without a shot fired. Along with Colonel William Prescott, Putnam argued for building a redoubt on Bunker Hill, the highest ground on the peninsula. Captain Knowlton sought to dissuade them by pointing out that British troops could land at the neck of the peninsula and cut off any supplies to the rebels occupying that ground; however, he agreed to participate if the decision was made to seize Bunker Hill.[56]

The men under Knowlton's command would be part of a larger force led by Colonel Prescott, who recalled: "On the 16 June, in the evening, I received orders to march to Breed's Hill in Charlestown, with a party of about one thousand men, consisting of three hundred of my own regiment, Colonel [John] Bridge and Lieut. [James] Brickett, with a detachment of theirs, and two hundred Connecticut forces, commanded by Captain Knowlton. We arrived at the spot, the lines were drawn by the engineer, and we began the intrenchment about twelve o'clock; and plying the work with all possible expedition till just before sun-rising, when the enemy began a very heavy cannonading and bombardment."[57]

By fashioning an earthen fort directly opposite the city held by His Majesty's regulars, the rebels committed themselves to a flagrant act of provocation that could not be ignored by General Gage without conceding the impotence of British rule over the province. And Gage did not. As he explained, "Preparations were instantly made for landing a body of men to drive them off, and ten companies of the grenadiers, ten of light-infantry, with the 5th, 38th, 43d, and 52d battalions, with a proportion of field artillery, under the command of Major-general Howe and Brigadier-general [Robert] Pigot, were embarked with great expedition, and landed on the peninsula without opposition, under the protection of some ships of war, armed vessels, and boats, by whose fire the rebels were kept within their works."[58]

Ordered by Prescott to oppose the advance of the British grenadiers and prevent them from outflanking the Breed's Hill redoubt, Knowlton's force took up a position on the eastern slope of the hill facing the Mystic River along a livestock fence that stretched for several hundred yards from the center of the peninsula nearly to the river. The captain's men reinforced the barrier with rails and posts taken from other fields while filling any openings with newly cut grass and hay, stones, sticks, and anything else available, to create a functional breastwork, from behind which they delivered a blistering musket fire at three lines of crack British troops. "Here they received the enemy to very tolerable advantage," according to Captain John Chester.[59] By one account, Knowlton walked along the breastwork in his shirt sleeves, cheering the defenders and firing his own musket until it was wrenched from his grasp by a cannon ball that bent the barrel so as to render it useless.[60]

Reinforced by two hundred men from the 2nd, 3rd, and 6th Connecticut Regiments, Knowlton's unit held firm until a general retreat was ordered. Then, functioning as a rearguard, they were among those providing protective cover when the entire rebel force withdrew from the field after depleting their ammunition. David Humphreys of Connecticut extolled the "deliberate and persevering valor" of these inexperienced soldiers, most of whom lacked bayonets, but noted the threat to those defending the redoubt on Breed's Hill when it fell, as "the light-infantry on their left would certainly have gained their rear, and exterminated this gallant corps, had not a body of four hundred Connecticut men, with the Captains Knowlton and Chester, after forming a temporary breast-work, by pulling up one post-and-rail fence and putting it upon another, performed prodigies of bravery. They held the enemy at bay until the main body had relinquished the heights, and then retreated across the Neck with more regularity, and less loss than could have been expected."[61]

Richard Frothingham's chronicle of the battle from 1873 reports that Knowlton earned "high praise" and elaborates on his role as follows: "General Putnam knew his merit, and selected him to command the fatigue party to accompany Colonel Prescott. He commenced the construction of the rail fence protection, and fought here with admirable bravery and conduct, until the retreat. He received from a Bostonian a gold-laced hat, a sash and gold breast-plate, for his behavior in this battle."[62]

The tableau of desperate fighting at Breed's Hill was recorded by one of the rebel combatants, upon whom the bloodshed left an indelible impression long afterward: "the scenes of carnage and death . . . appear as vivid as if the events of yesterday."[63] The defenders exacted a heavy price, causing one British officer to lament that "from an absurd and destructive confidence, carelessness or ignorance, we have lost a thousand of our best men and officers and have given the rebels great matter of triumph by showing them what mischief they can do us."[64] The tally of redcoat dead and wounded on June 17 exceeded American casualties by more than two-to-one, and General Gage confessed: "The loss we have sustained is greater than we can bear."[65] He was recalled to London and departed in October, leaving General Howe in charge of British land forces in America.

THE RAID AT CHARLESTOWN

Knowlton's performance at Bunker Hill caught the attention of many, including the Continental Army's new commander-in-chief, and would lead to promotion. He was nominated for major at a council of war held by Washington and his generals at army headquarters in Cambridge on November 2, 1775, and named to that rank in Colonel Benedict Arnold's 20th Continental Regiment on January 1, 1776. On that date, the former 3rd Connecticut was reorganized and rededicated with its new numerical designation as part of a broader reorganization of the army. Arnold's absence, arising from his participation in the Canadian campaign that winter, left Lieutenant Colonel John Durkee and Major Knowlton in charge of the regiment.

On January 8, the newly minted major, on orders from Washington, led some two hundred men in a successful raid that set fire to several houses still standing in Charlestown—those that had escaped the flames sparked by cannon fire during the

Breed's Hill battle—in order to prevent their being occupied by British patrols or used as firewood by the redcoats. The attackers crossed over to Charlestown from the American position on Cobble Hill and struck between eight and nine in the evening. Employing the stealth and daring reminiscent of the ranger tactics Knowlton had learned in the last war, the rebel foray largely accomplished its mission while barely firing a shot and without losing a single man.

The commander-in-chief described the action to Joseph Reed several days later: "We made a successful attempt a few Nights ago upon the Houses near Bunker Hill—A Party under Majr Knolton crossd upon the Mill damn [the milldam paralleled Charlestown Neck a few hundred yards to the southwest and provided a direct route to Bunker Hill from Cobble Hill] (the Night being Dark) and set fire to, and burnt down Eight, out of 14 which were standing, and which we found they were daily pulling down for Fuel— five Soldiers, & the Wife of one of them, Inhabiting one of the Houses, were brought of Prisoners; another Soldier was killed; none of ours hurt."[66] Washington reported to John Hancock that the attackers crossed the milldam "about half after eight ô clock, & gallantly executed their business," capturing "a Serjeant and four privates of the 10th Regiment."[67]

The other side's response to this intrusion created a far greater clamor than did the raiders. Writing to his friend Mercy Otis Warren from his Braintree home that night, John Adams—on leave from congressional duties in Philadelphia—recounted what he saw and heard of the affair: "A very hot Fire both of Artillery and small Arms has continued for half an Hour, and has been succeded by a luminous Phoenomenon, over Braintree North Common occasioned by Burning Buildings I suppose."[68] The redcoats did virtually all the shooting, according to Washington, as Knowlton's force encountered "but one man more there who makeing Some resistance, they were obliged to dispatch—the gun that Killd him, was the only one that was discharged by our men, tho Severall hundreds were fired by the enemy from within their works, but in So Confused a manner that not one of our people was hurt."[69]

In his general orders the following day, Washington thanked the colonel "and the Officers and Soldiers, who were under his command last night; for the Spirit, Conduct and Secrecy, with which they burnt the Houses, near the Enemy's works, upon Bunkers-hill—The General was in a more particular manner pleased, with the resolution the party discover'd in not firing a Shot; as nothing betrays greater signs of fear, and less of the soldier, than to begin a loose, undirected and unmeaning Fire, from whence no good can result, nor any valuable purposes answer'd."[70]

Knowlton's raid created a considerable disturbance among British troops and Loyalist civilians in Boston, as it disrupted the premiere of a satirical play allegedly written by General John Burgoyne entitled *The Blockade of Boston* and attended by uniformed officers and their ladies at Faneuil Hall. Because Boston had no theater, General Howe had arranged to have this venue converted into a playhouse for amateur productions of Shakespeare and original farces in which officers and favored citizens acted.[71] According to Lieutenant Martin Hunter of the British Light Infantry, then posted in the redoubt at Charlestown, the Patriot army knew when the play was to be performed and timed its attack to coincide with "the very hour that the farce began." In the ensuing confusion, the king's soldiers launched a volley to no purpose: "Not a man of the enemy was within three miles of us, and the party that came along the milldam had effected their object and carried off the sergeant's guard. However, our firing caused a general alarm at Boston, and all the troops got under arms." If Knowlton's men aimed "to put a stop to the farce for the evening, they certainly succeeded, as all the officers immediately left the playhouse and joined the regiments." Even more farcical was the difficulty a British orderly sergeant had convincing the audience at Faneuil Hall that he was not merely acting a part in the play when he ascended the stage to announce news of the American raid.[72]

A NEW ROLE

Two and a half months later, General Howe's army evacuated Boston under threat from American artillery newly positioned on

Dorchester Heights and retired to Halifax in preparation for launching its New York campaign. As Washington's forces moved south to counter the anticipated threat, Knowlton had time to briefly visit his family in Ashford—the last time he would see home. A new challenge awaited him once he and his regiment joined the rest of the army on Manhattan Island, for the commanding general intended to utilize the skills Knowlton had learned in the last war to enhance the Continental Army's intelligence-gathering capability.

Washington was keenly aware of the value of military intelligence from his earliest days as a soldier leading Virginia provincials against the French and their Indian confederates. In a letter to the governor of Pennsylvania, Robert Hunter Morris, on January 1, 1756, the young colonel assured the former of his diligent attention to this concern in opposing an adversary engaged in the stealthy tactics of wilderness warfare: "There is nothing *more* necessary than good intelligence to frustrate a designing Enemy: and nothing that requires greater pains to obtain. I shall therefore chearfully come into any measures you can propose to settle a correspondence for this salutary end: and you may depend upon receiving (when the provinces are threatened) the earliest and best intelligence I can procure."[73]

As commander of the Continental Army, Washington was more focused than ever on the need for accurate information about the number, position, and movement of enemy troops. His insatiable appetite for those details led him to Knowlton, whose abilities had impressed the commander-in-chief for some time and who enjoyed the reputation of being an experienced hand at gathering such information from his service with the ranger companies led by Robert Rogers and Israel Putnam. Major Aaron Burr, General Putnam's aide, evidently shared the high opinion of Knowlton that prevailed among others who knew him. He is said to have remarked years later, "It was impossible to promote such a man too rapidly."[74]

The farmer from Ashford advanced in rank again when Congress, upon the Board of War's recommendation, resolved that he be commissioned lieutenant colonel of the 20th Continental

Regiment, commanded by Colonel John Durkee, on August 10, 1776. At Washington's direction, the newly promoted officer formed a contingent known as "Knowlton's Rangers" or the "Connecticut Rangers," which comprised about 130 soldiers from Connecticut, Massachusetts, and Rhode Island. They were drawn from five Continental regiments and one state unit. Knowlton appears to have selected officers he knew for the Rangers, a large proportion of whom were from Connecticut. They included: Major Andrew Colburn; Adjutant Thomas Fosdick; four captains; seven lieutenants; and four ensigns, among them Daniel Knowlton, Thomas's older brother. Fifteen-year-old Frederick Knowlton, a private in Durkee's 20th Connecticut, accompanied his father into service with the Rangers.[75]

Regarded as an elite unit, Knowlton's men assumed the role of a light infantry and skirmishing force whose primary purpose was to meet Washington's desperate need for information about the British army opposing him, he being "extremely anxious to learn the strength and contemplated movements of the enemy."[76] Although scouting remained the Rangers' strong suit, they were expected to take on any mission that was especially hazardous or required an unusual degree of individual initiative to accomplish.[77] That is to say, their function was to embrace the hardships and dangers that had attended Rogers's Rangers, and in which Knowlton was steeped from the last war.

Washington's lack of information about enemy troop totals and dispositions prior to and during the Battle of Long Island had eventuated in a near-catastrophe for his army and convinced him he needed a singular force dedicated to this purpose, which would report directly to the commander-in-chief. Knowlton and his Rangers were given no opportunity to conduct reconnaissance in advance of that engagement as they had only arrived at Brooklyn Heights the day before; they included one hundred Connecticut Continentals who were the nucleus of the Rangers and found themselves among the last American troops to cross the East River from Manhattan.[78] Some of them narrowly escaped capture on August 27.[79]

Washington's letter of September 6 to General William Heath reflected his sense of the urgent need to ascertain enemy intentions: "As every thing in a manner depends upon obtaining intelligence of the enemy's motions, I do most earnestly entreat you and General [George] Clinton to exert yourselves to accomplish this most desirable end. Leave no stone unturned, nor do not stick at expense to bring this to pass, as I never was more uneasy than on account of my want of knowledge on this score." From his headquarters in New York City, the commander-in-chief further urged: "Keep, besides this precaution, constant lookouts (with good glasses) on some commanding heights that look well on to the other shore (and especially into the bays, where boats can be concealed), that they may observe, more particularly in the evening, if there be any uncommon movements. Much will depend upon early intelligence, and meeting the enemy before they can intrench. I should much approve of small harassing parties, stealing, as it were, over in the night, as they might keep the enemy alarmed, and more than probably bring off a prisoner, from whom some valuable intelligence may be obtained."[80]

NATHAN HALE

On the heels of the August 27 debacle, Washington turned to Knowlton to secure a volunteer from among his Rangers for a special scouting service to obtain accurate information about the enemy's strength and positions on British-occupied Long Island. Knowlton would inadvertently create a legendary hero by accepting one volunteer's offer to undertake the mission ordered by Washington. Because no one could be ordered to embark on so perilous a journey, the colonel called a meeting of his officers on September 10 to find someone willing to go behind British lines, but only one man agreed to do so—twenty-one-year-old Captain Nathan Hale, former schoolmaster in East Haddam and then New London who had enlisted in 1775 and been invited to join the Rangers after distinguishing himself by capturing a small supply-laden vessel from under the guns of a British man-of-war.[81] He offered Knowlton his services as a spy after Lieutenant James Sprague, a veteran of the French and Indian War, refused to engage in espionage on the grounds that "he was ready to fight at any time or place however dangerous but never could consent to expose himself to be hung like a dog."[82]

As his friend Captain William Hull recalled, Hale responded affirmatively to Knowlton's solicitation because "he thought he owed to his country the accomplishment of an object so important, and so much desired by the Commander of her armies, and he knew of no other mode of obtaining the information, than by assuming a disguise and passing into the enemy's camp."[83]

Regrettably, the youthful captain, who was described as "peculiarly free from the shadow of guile . . . however imperious circumstances of personal safety might demand a resort to duplicity & ambiguity," was temperamentally ill-suited to such an endeavor.[84] Aside from having a personality that was too open for clandestine activity, the teacher-turned-spy had no relevant experience or training, and the notes and drawings he would make and carry behind enemy lines guaranteed his conviction if captured. It is a measure of how dire Washington's need for intelligence was that he would have assigned this task to someone so unprepared to carry it out. (Adding to the futility of Hale's mission was the fact that the purpose for which Washington had conceived it, to obtain information about the disposition and objective of British forces on Long Island, was obviated by their landing at Kip's Bay on September 15.)

Departing the American encampment at Harlem Heights during the second week of September, Hale crossed to Long Island dressed as a schoolmaster. There he was captured by the British on September 21. The prisoner was brought before General Howe at his Manhattan headquarters in the house of James Beekman near the East River (at the corner of First Avenue and Fifty-first Street today), and Sir William ordered that he be executed as a spy the following day without benefit of a trial. (Howe was no doubt incensed at the suspected but never-proven arson by rebel sympathizers on the night of September 20–21 that left much of British-occupied New York City smoldering, but it is reasonable to assume his verdict would have been the same even had there been no such fire, given that Hale readily confessed to the purpose of his mission and was found with incriminating documents on his person.) The next morning, Hale met his fate at the nearby artillery park. Captain Frederick MacKenzie of the Royal Welch Fusiliers recorded that the condemned man "behaved with great composure and resolution, saying he thought it the duty of every good Officer, to obey any orders given him by his Commander-in-Chief; and desired the Spectators to be at all times prepared to meet death in whatever shape it might appear."[85] It is a matter of conjecture whether Hale actually spoke the line from Joseph Addison's play *Cato* that has been ever since attributed to him: "I only regret, that I have but one life to lose for my country."[86]

In one of his last acts, Hale dashed off a report to Knowlton that was included among the two letters he wrote that morning, unaware that the tides of war had overtaken his superior officer just six days before.[87] When the king's forces landed at Kip's Bay on September 15, the Rangers were posted along the Harlem shore—where the expected enemy strike failed to materialize—and thus played no role in the day's events. The next morning, however, they would be thrust into the center of action.

THREE

Reconnaissance
and Resistance

PRELUDE

The American troops who joined their comrades on Harlem
Heights on the evening of Sunday, September 15, 1776, after a
disorderly flight up Manhattan Island, were reeling from the day's
woeful sequence of events and largely in a despondent mood—
exhausted, cold, hungry, and in some cases ashamed at failing to
resist the Anglo-German invaders.

The near-disaster they suffered has been attributed to three
immediate factors that reflected a failure of command. First, un-
seasoned soldiers should not have been tasked with defending
the landing grounds at Kip's Bay. Second, their physical defenses
were wholly inadequate against the enemy assault. And third, the
Americans manifested an appalling lack of leadership at all levels
throughout the day.[1] This perspective challenges the derisive as-
sessment by Nathanael Greene that would seem to exculpate his
fellow officers from any responsibility for the rueful turn of

events: "We made a miserable disorderly Retreat from New York, owing to the disorderly conduct of the Militia who run at the appearance of the Enemies Advance Guard."[2] Perhaps Greene forgot what he had written to John Adams not long before: "Good Officers is the very Soul of an Army; the activity and Zeal of the Troops entirely depends upon the degree of animation given them by their officers."[3]

Benjamin Trumbull of the Connecticut militia would have undoubtedly agreed with Greene's latter observation. Deploring the lack of artillery to resist the Crown's forces when they came ashore and the absence of reinforcements from rebel troops on the upper island, he defended the actions of the common soldiers in lower Manhattan who sought to elude the enemy and reach the safety of Harlem Heights: "In such a Situation it was not reasonable to expect that they would make any vigorous Stand. The men were blamed for retreating and even flying in these Circumstances, but I imagine the fault was principally in the General Officers in not disposing of things so as to give the men a rational prospect of Defence and a Safe retreat should they engage the Enemy. And it is probable many Lives were saved, and much to the Army prevented in their coming off as y^y did tho' it was not honourable. It is admirable that so few men are lost."[4]

Private Joseph Plumb Martin agreed that the Continental officers had failed those they led: "every man that I saw was endeavouring by all sober means to escape from death or captivity, which, at that period of the war was almost certain death." Martin was presumably alluding to the British prison ships on which those confined died at an alarming rate. "The men were confused, being without officers to command them;—I do not recollect of seeing a commissioned officer from the time I left the lines on the banks of the East River, in the morning, until I met with the *gentlemanly* one in the evening." This is a sarcastic reference to an officer who detained Martin and a sick comrade whom he was assisting near sundown, until the officer's attention was diverted by another soldier, which enabled Martin and his friend to proceed on their way. "How could the men fight without officers?"[5]

Even Colonel Henry Knox, when writing to his brother, argued the need for a more reliable officer corps to support Washington: "The general is as worthy a man as breathes, but he cannot do every thing nor be everywhere. He wants good assistants. There is a radical evil in our army,—the lack of officers. We ought to have men of merit in the most extensive and unlimited sense of the word. Instead of which, the bulk of the officers of the army are a parcel of ignorant, stupid men, who might make tolerable soldiers, but [are] bad officers; and until Congress forms an establishment to induce men proper for the purpose to leave their usual employments and enter the service, it is ten to one they will be beat till they are heartily tired of it."[6]

Captain David Humphreys, who had accompanied General Israel Putnam's column that barely escaped the redcoats during their trek up the west side of the island from the city late on the 15th, described their pitiable circumstances: "That night our soldiers, excessively fatigued by the sultry march of the day, their clothes wet by a severe shower of rain that succeeded towards the evening, their blood chilled by the cold wind that produced a sudden change in the temperature of the air, and their hearts sunk within them by the loss of baggage, artillery, and works in which they had been taught to put great confidence, lay upon their arms, covered only by the clouds of an uncomfortable sky."[7]

With the evacuation from lower Manhattan, the number of soldiers stationed on the Harlem high ground had doubled from the previous night, and many were forced to sleep in the open without tents, which were among the supplies left behind during their hurried departure from the city.[8] In addition, none of the officers or rank and file, including the army's commander, could be confident that the next day would not bring a renewed assault. Captain Samuel Richards of Connecticut recalled: "We were employed principally thro' the succeeding night in throwing up a slight entrenchment on the brow of the hill called Haerlem heights, in full expectation of being attacked by the enemy in the morning."[9]

About ten thousand troops were now gathered within the fortified lines on the Harlem bluffs, with another six thousand to the north at King's Bridge under General William Heath; however, less than half of the aggregate total were Continental regulars, who had enlisted for the year. The rest were state levies serving for six months or local militia serving for three months.[10] Washington had planned for three parallel defensive lines running west to east and stretching from present-day 125th Street north to 160th Street, while a garrison was stationed at Fort Washington overlooking the Hudson River further up the island. According to Philip Vickers Fithian's journal entry late Sunday, written at the encampment on the heights, "Gen. Washington came up to the lines before Night; viewed them, & how they were manned, with much Attention."[11] The imminent danger and spectacle of combat were understandably on the writer's mind: "There is something forceably grand in the Sound of Drums & Fifes, when they are calling such an Army as ours to contend with another of perhaps equal Force! Whenever they come together the Death of many must be the Consequence—And this Thought with all its Pomp of serious Grandieur, is ever associated with the Call to Arms when the two Armies lie so near each other, & daily expect an Action!"[12]

Having assigned his brigades to their posts, Washington had done what he could to prepare for any resumption of fighting on Monday. He knew the initiative rested with the British and that should they attack, disaster loomed if the American troops' will to fight was no more evident than it had been on the 15th. Still, the commander-in-chief reasoned that by defending the heights, even against the advice of some of his generals who feared encirclement in northern Manhattan by the Crown's forces, the rebel army would enjoy the advantages of natural strength that the elevated terrain afforded against a superior adversary. This, the general hoped, would enable them to secure a victory, even a token one, and provide a sorely needed boost to his soldiers' morale— if only they would fight rather than run.[13] Meanwhile, Washington had set the men on the rocky plateau to work with picks and spades, and they would be feverishly digging entrenchments in the days ahead.

Figure 1. *The Death of General Warren at the Battle of Bunker's Hill, June 17, 1775* by John Trumbull. Dr. Joseph Warren lies mortally wounded in the foreground just to the left of center, cradled by an unknown militiaman in bare feet seeking to avert a grenadier's bayonet with his left arm and with Thomas Knowlton, then a captain with the 5th Company of the 3rd Connecticut Regiment under General Israel Putnam, standing over them. (*Museum of Fine Arts, Boston*)

Figure 2. *George Washington* by Charles Willson Peale, 1776. Washington was
the obvious choice when in June 1775 the Continental Congress appointed a
commander-in-chief of the new American army. As a Southerner and resident
of the largest colony, Virginia, it was hoped his selection would generate support beyond New England for the colonial rebellion against Great Britain.
Seeking to recover from his errors of judgment at the Battle of Long Island
on August 27, 1776, Washington led the near-miraculous evacuation of American forces from Brooklyn Heights and launched a maneuver that attempted
to outflank the enemy at the Battle of Harlem Heights on September 16, 1776.
(*White House Collection*)

CHARLES Earl CORNWALLIS Lieu. Gen.
And Col. of the 33 Regim.t of Foot

Figure 3. *Charles Earl Cornwallis, Lieu. Gen. and Col. of the 33rd Regiment of Foot.*
Cornwallis was the most aristocratic of His Majesty's generals serving in America and one of the few British officers to study at a military academy. During the Battle of Harlem Heights, he commanded the Corps de Reserve that moved to reinforce the Crown's troops engaged in the action, although it did not actually join in the fighting. Along with Major General John Vaughan, Cornwallis led the British grenadiers who came ashore in the first wave of Anglo-German troops at Kip's Bay the day before. (*New York Public Library*)

The HON.BLE S.R W.M HOWE.

Knight of the Bath, & Commander in Chief of his Majesty's Forces in America.

LONDON:Published as the Act directs, 10th Nov'r 1777, by JOHN MORRIS, Rathbone Place.

Figure 4. *The Honorable Sir William Howe* by Richard Purcell, 1777. Commander of the British land forces in America in 1776, Major General Howe led the most powerful military expedition Britain had ever sent beyond Europe and the largest it had deployed anywhere for several decades. In his typically un-hurried manner, Howe waited seventeen days before invading Manhattan after his tactical success at the Battle of Long Island. His older brother, Admiral Richard Lord Howe, commanded the fleet that dominated the waters around New York. (*Anne S. K. Brown Military History Collection, Brown University Library*)

Figure 5. *Sir Henry Clinton, Knight of the Bath & Commander in Chief in America
&c.*, c. 1778. The son of a former Royal Governor of New York, Lieutenant
General Clinton was regarded as the most cerebral of the British generals in
America. He proposed the flanking maneuver along the Jamaica Pass that was
key to the victory at the Battle of Long Island and commanded the first wave
of the Anglo-German invasion force that landed at Kip's Bay (the site of Manhattan's Thirty-fourth Street today) on September 15, 1776. (*Anne S. K. Brown
Military History Collection, Brown University Library*)

Figure 6. *Alexander Leslie.* Brigadier General Leslie was an able and respected officer who commanded the British light infantry engaged at the Battle of Harlem Heights. They were in the first wave of the invasion force that landed at Kip's Bay on September 15, 1776. (*New York Public Library*)

Figure 7. *Major General Nathanael Greene* by Charles Willson Peale, 1783. Greene, only thirty-four when the war started and the product of a prominent Rhode Island family, deviated from his Quaker roots to embrace the Continental Army and impressed Washington with his talent for organizational efficiency. He experienced his first taste of battle at Harlem Heights, where he commanded a division comprised of troops from Massachusetts, Rhode Island, and Maryland. (*Independence National Historical Park*)

ISRAEL PUTNAM Esqr.

MAJOR GENERAL of the Connecticut Forces, and COMMANDER in CHIEF at the Engagement on BUNCKERS HILL near BOSTON, 17 June 1775.

Figure 8. *Israel Putnam.* Major General Putnam, a veteran of the French and Indian War who served with Thomas Knowlton during that conflict, was the third general (after Nathanael Greene and Thomas Sullivan) chosen by Washington to lead the ill-fated effort to resist the enemy assault at Long Island. He supervised the army's evacuation of New York City on September 15, 1776, and commanded a division that fought at Harlem Heights the next day. (*Anne S. K. Brown Collection, Brown University Library*)

Figure 9. *Thomas Knowlton.* This image is based on John Trumbull's depiction of him in his painting of the Battle of Bunker Hill. Knowlton compiled a remarkable record of service to the Revolution before being mortally wounded at the Battle of Harlem Heights. Knowlton's Rangers, the forerunner of the U.S. Army's intelligence branch, brought on that engagement with their early morning reconnaissance mission, and Washington paid tribute to the fallen colonel afterwards as one "who would have been an honor to any Country." (*Alamy Stock Photo, AR Collection*)

Figure 10. *Kepp's [Kip's] Bay 17th Augt. 1778 where the troops landed 15th Septr. 1776. Phoenix 44 Capt. H. Parker, Roebuck 44 Hammond. Carisford 28 Fanshaw. Rose 20 Js. Wallace. 12th Augt. 1778.* This image of Kip's Bay and the East River is a sketch by Archibald Robertson, who witnessed the landing of Anglo-German troops there on September 15, 1776. (*New York Public Library*)

Figure 11. *The Battle of Harlem Heights*, a nineteenth-century print engraved by James Charles Armytage based on the *Battle of Harlem* by Alonzo Chappel (1859), depicts the 42nd (Royal Highland) Regiment of Foot—known as "The Black Watch"—retreating under American fire. (*Anne S. K. Brown Collection, Brown University Library*)

Figure 12. This view of the field where the principal action was fought at the Battle of Harlem Heights is looking north from One Hundred and Sixteenth Street, with Barnard College in the center near where the buckwheat field stood in 1776. Columbia University is on the right, with Bloomingdale Road on the left along the line of trees and Grant's Tomb in the background. From *The Battle of Harlem Heights, September 16, 1776* by Henry P. Johnston, 1897.

Figure 13. This is a view of the rocky elevation north of One Hundred and Twenty-third Street where Knowlton's flanking attack occurred during the Battle of Harlem Heights. Grant's Tomb is in the background. From *The Battle of Harlem Heights* by Henry P. Johnston, 1897.

Figure 14. This bronze statue of Thomas Knowlton by Enoch Smith Woods has been standing guard at the Connecticut State Capitol in Hartford since 1895. Its facial features are based on the image of Knowlton in John Trumbull's painting of the Battle of Bunker Hill. (*Alamy Stock Photo, History and Art Collection*)

On the other side, General Howe had completed the first day of his Manhattan offensive by occupying New York City with part of his force and sending the rest northward to establish a line across the island one mile below Harlem Heights. In order to parry a possible British thrust at the American lines on the high ground, Washington positioned two divisions near the center of the ridge, one led by General Putnam and the other by Major General Joseph Spencer, and General Greene's division on the southern slopes—where any enemy advance would make first contact with the defenders—opposite a small valley known as the Hollow Way (near today's 125th Street), which stretched west toward the Hudson shoreline. Here the island narrowed into a panhandle between the Hudson and Harlem Rivers with both waterways extending northward to King's Bridge on the Spuyten Duyvil Creek. Greene's troops included the brigades of Brigadier General John Nixon and Colonel Paul Dudley Sargent, and Brigadier General Reazin Beall's militia.[14] Except for Beall's Marylanders, Greene's force comprised New Englanders from Massachusetts and Rhode Island.

THE PROBE

In the wake of his army's dreadful performance on September 15, Washington could have been forgiven if his last thought upon going to bed that night, or his first thought when awakening the next day, had been to rue his acceptance of Congress's offer to command the Continental Army. The decision to assume that burden stemmed, at least in part, from an insistent sense of personal obligation that was inextricable from a focus on how others perceived him, or so he claimed in a letter to his wife Martha two days after being chosen by Congress: "it was utterly out of my power to refuse this appointment without exposing my Character to such censures as would have reflected dishonour upon myself, and given pain to my friends—this I am sure could not, and ought not to be pleasing to you, & must have lessened me considerably in my own esteem."[15] It has even been suggested that the proprietor of the Mount Vernon estate was so obsessed with his social standing as a country squire that he was less unsettled at the prospect of death in battle or being hanged as a rebel traitor by the British than at the thought someone would fairly accuse him of failing to fulfill the obligations of a gentleman.[16]

Notwithstanding that he may have been plagued with gnawing self-doubts at this moment, Washington sat down in the early morning hours of the 16th at the Roger Morris house to write John Hancock about the army's circumstances. Throughout the war, he would spend far more time drafting correspondence than commanding men in battle, but on this day he did both. The commander-in-chief explained: "We are now encamped with the Main body of the Army on the Heights of Harlem where I should hope the Enemy would meet with a defeat in case of an Attack, If the Generality of our Troops would behave with tolerable bravery, but experience to my extreme affliction has convinced me that this is rather to be wished for than expected; However I trust, that there are many who will act like men, and shew themselves worthy of the blessings of Freedom." Washington advised Hancock that he had "sent out some reconoitring parties to gain Intelligence If possible of the disposition of the Enemy and shall inform Congress of every material event by the earliest Opportunity."[17]

Knowlton's Rangers were the "reconoitring parties" to which Washington alluded. He had no way of knowing that the British were not planning to renew their assault that day and so had ordered Knowlton to conduct a reconnaissance of the enemy's position and report any movements. The general needed to determine whether General Howe's left wing along the Bloomingdale Road was digging in or preparing to attack, but the view in that direction from his headquarters at Roger Morris's house was obscured by thick woods. This was in contrast to the clear field of vision he enjoyed to the east where Harlem Plains lay, so that he could easily detect any approach by the British right wing from McGowan's Pass.[18]

The Rangers moved out before dawn and worked their way south toward enemy lines.[19] With Knowlton leading the way, they ventured quietly down the bluffs and across the Hollow Way, then up the hill to its south that is today the site of Columbia University, Barnard College, and the Cathedral of St. John the Divine, and ends on the east at Morningside Heights. The Rangers had never before been in battle as a unit, having spent the previous day near Harlem awaiting an attack at Hell Gate that never occurred, but they were in good spirits and eager for action.[20]

At about sunrise, Knowlton's party was spotted by British pickets (stationed at about today's 104th Street and Broadway) while advancing through the fields near Nicholas Jones's stone farmhouse west of the Bloomingdale Road (on what is now 106th Street between West End Avenue and Riverside Drive), and this locale would mark the southernmost point of the fighting to come.[21] The Jones house was one of three in the area whose property would be encompassed by the forthcoming engagement. The other two—Adrian Hoaglandt's at the end of the Bloomingdale Road (now 115th Street and Riverside Drive) and to its east Harman Vandewater's (at what is now 114th Street near today's Mount Sinai Morningside hospital)—were the only houses on the high ground later known as Bloomingdale Heights and now as Morningside Heights.[22]

According to General Howe, "The position the King's army took, on the 15th in the evening, was with the right to Horen's Hook, and the left at the North River near to Bloomingdale."[23] The pickets whom Knowlton's Rangers encountered were the advance guard on the extreme left of Howe's troop alignment. They were encamped near the New Bloomingdale Crossroad in what is now Central Park, on the line of Ninety-first to Ninety-sixth Street, a short distance from the home of Charles Apthorpe (which stood until 1891). Apthorpe's mansion (just south of the Crossroad or what is now Ninety-first Street and slightly west of Ninth Avenue) anchored the end of an Anglo-German line that extended to the island's eastern shore.[24]

After landing at Kip's Bay, the Crown's soldiers had marched up the island with only their weapons, provisions, and blankets, and were forced to find whatever accommodations they could that night, in some cases retrieving knapsacks and other equipment left behind in the defenders' flight.[25] George Harris, a captain with the 5th Regiment's grenadier company, recounted his experience: "After landing in York Island, we drove the Americans into their works beyond the eight mile-stone from New York, and thus got possession of the best half of the island. We took post opposite to them, placed our picquets, borrowed a sheep, killed, cooked, and ate some of it and then went up to sleep on a gate, which we took the liberty of throwing off its hinges, covering our feet with an American tent, for which we should have cut poles and pitched, had it not been so dark."[26]

Upon detecting Knowlton's scouts at daybreak on the 16th, the redcoat pickets near Nicholas Jones's farmhouse fired their guns to alert the nearest units, encamped several hundred yards to the south—the 2nd and 3rd Battalions of General Leslie's light infantry and the 42nd (Royal Highland) Regiment of Foot, known as "The Black Watch" and consisting almost entirely of soldiers from Scotland.[27] Feared more by Washington's troops than any other enemy combatants, except for the Hessians, the Black Watch were chosen for their imposing height. They carried broadswords and daggers in addition to their muskets and bayonets, wore short scarlet coats and kilts with their famous regimental tartans, and marched to the skirl of bagpipes and the beat of drums.[28]

Knowlton's men were supposed to be scouting rather than fighting, but they stood their ground rather than scatter when the pickets took shots at them—a far cry from the behavior exhibited by most Patriot troops the day before. The Rangers returned fire and after several rounds sought cover behind a low stone wall on the Jones farm. The Battle of Harlem Heights had begun.

With admirable efficiency, a column of about four hundred redcoats—elements of two or three different companies—came up the Bloomingdale Road in prompt response to the pickets' alert. Employing the tactical insights accrued from his days as a ranger in the previous war, Knowlton called his soldiers' attention to a point on the road fifty yards south of Jones's stone wall (at about 107th Street today). According to Private Oliver Burnham, then not quite sixteen years of age, "The Colonel marked a place about eight or ten rods from the wall and charged us not to raise or fire a gun until the enemy's front reached that place. The British followed in Solid column and soon were on the ground designated," when Knowlton gave the order to fire.[29] In response, Leslie's light infantry formed a firing line and both sides blasted away at each other for half an hour, standing almost face to face and holding their positions while discharging their firearms as fast as they could reload them. In most cases, this was the English flintlock musket known as the Brown Bess employed by the majority in both armies, although some Rangers were equipped with rifles.[30]

The king's regulars relied on the Brown Bess, which was carried by many American soldiers in units other than rifle companies, as the use of this weapon—while known for its limited range—enabled the Britons' favored tactic of the bayonet charge. The lead ball fired from a Brown Bess was about three-quarters of an inch in diameter and weighed just over an ounce. It was able to smash and penetrate bones, organs, and tissue, and could kill or injure at a distance of up to three hundred yards; however, because of inherent inaccuracy and unreliable loading, the musket's effective range was only between fifty and eighty yards, and shooting at anything more than a hundred yards away was foolhardy. Ultimately, only 5 percent of all musket balls fired at another soldier hit their mark.[31] But those that did could have a devastating impact. Unlike the smaller rifle bullet that tended to pass through its target, a musket ball usually remained inside the body, enveloped by the lacerated flesh or organs it penetrated.[32]

During the half-hour clash between the Rangers and redcoats, both were able to fire eight rounds apiece (about a thousand total on each side); and the twenty casualties sustained, mostly wounded, were divided equally between them. The skirmish was broken up when Knowlton, observing the advance of the Black Watch that threatened his flank, ordered a retreat. His men made an orderly withdrawal, relying on the ranger-like tactics that were part of Robert Rogers's woodlands-warfare protocol in order to protect their rear and foil the attempted flanking maneuver. Each took turns firing to cover the other, and they fell back along a route that roughly corresponded with the Bloomingdale Road while using both sides of the highway, chased by the light infantry even as the Black Watch halted their advance. The Rangers proceeded north to the end of the Bloomingdale Road at the Hoaglandt farmhouse and then entered the Hollow Way. Leslie's regulars pursued Knowlton's men for more than a mile until reaching a rise known as Claremont (a few hundred yards north of where Grant's Tomb stands today). As their elusive prey dashed across the valley and ascended the bluffs to reunite with Greene's brigades, the scarlet-clad combatants paused to catch their breath and presumably savor their moment of triumph.[33] This was the third time in three weeks that they had sent the rebels running.

In his iconic narrative of the battle, Henry P. Johnston sought to infer Knowlton's mindset from the brief stand made by his Rangers during this opening phase of the engagement: "Knowlton, although dangerously near the enemy's position, bravely stood his ground for a time. He seemed to feel that there had been running enough the day before, and called upon his men to prove their mettle. It would be something to show the Light Infantry soldiers especially that panics did not last over night. As the Rangers had been chosen to meet such situations as this, they did not disappoint their leader."[34] Johnston's conjecture aside, the flurry of decisions the colonel was required to make in this encounter were arguably informed less by his perception of the prior day's events than by more elemental considerations: his conception of how to fight and his commitment to a cause. This was Knowlton at his best, managing the kind of stubborn resistance against a superior force that had earned him plaudits at Bunker Hill. To be sure, his mission was to scout and not engage the enemy, but everything in his record signaled that if a fight developed, he would be loath to run away without making at least a defiant gesture.

One of the Ranger officers, probably Captain Stephen Brown of Woodstock, Connecticut—who had been drawn from Durkee's 20th Connecticut Regiment—provided an account of the initial skirmish to a friend in New London, Connecticut, several days later: "Well, on Monday Morning the General [Washington] ordered us to go and take the Enemy's advanced Guard; accordingly we set out just before Day, and found where they were; at Day-brake we were discovered by the Enemy, who were 400 strong, and we were 120." The light infantry "march'd up within six Rods of us, and there form'd to give us Battle which we were ready for; and Colonel Knowlton gave Orders to fire, which we did, and stood theirs till we perceived they were getting their Flank-Guards round us. After giving them eight Rounds a Piece the Colonel gave Orders for Retreating, which we performed very well, without the Loss of a Man while Retreating, though we lost about 10 while in Action."[35]

ACTION AND REACTION

When word reached the Morris house at about seven a.m. of the Rangers' encounter, the news was scanty. While conversing with his adjutant general, Joseph Reed, Washington received a message that musket fire had been heard to the southwest. With the commander-in-chief's leave, Colonel Reed rode south to ascertain the situation and reached the Rangers just before the shooting started, as he described in a letter to his wife the following day: "an Acct. [account] came that the Enemy were advancing upon us in three large Columns—we have so many false Reports that I desired the General to permit me to go & discover what Truth there was in the Acct. I accordingly went down to our most advanced Guard & while I was talking with the Officer [presumably Knowlton], the Enemy's advanced Guard fired upon us at a small Distance." Reed complimented the Rangers on their performance against a larger foe: "our men behaved well stood & return'd the Fire till overpowered by numbers they were obliged to retreat—the Enemy advanced upon us very fast; I had not quitted a House [presumably the Hoaglandt farmhouse] 5 minutes before they were in Possession of it—Finding how things were going

I went over to the General to get some support for the brave Fellows who had behaved so well."[36]

The preliminary skirmish between the Rangers and light infantry not only led to the main engagement that day but also entailed certain general movements and preparatory activity within the American encampment. For one thing, it immediately put the advance guard on the heights on alert as it had done with the British; soldiers hastened to their posts in anticipation of going into action or repelling an attack.[37] Washington put his main force in readiness, that being Putnam's and Spencer's divisions stationed north of Greene's; most of those troops were positioned along the line of today's 147th Street where the first entrenchments were thrown up across Manhattan Island. The work on these defenses began during Knowlton's skirmish with the light infantry. Colonel Gold Selleck Silliman of the Connecticut militia described what occurred while writing to his wife the next day: "Yesterday at 7 o'clock in the morning we were alarmed with the sight of a considerable number of the enemy on the Plains below us about a mile distant.—Our Brigades which form a line across the Island where I am were immediately ordered under arms— but as the enemy did not immediately advance we grounded our arms & took spades & shovels and went to work & before night had thrown up lines across the Island—There was nothing before but three little redoubts in about a mile & we are at work this day in strengthening them."[38]

After Reed had left Washington to investigate the state of affairs arising from the Rangers' skirmish, the general and some aides rode two miles from the Morris house at the northern end of the American encampment down to its southernmost point so that Washington could view for himself the action on Greene's immediate front. Reed reported to the commander-in-chief shortly before nine a.m., after having conferred briefly with Knowlton. He advised Washington that the Rangers had acquitted themselves well in their encounter with the British advance guard, even if they had exceeded their intelligence-gathering mission. Reed urged Washington to dispatch reinforcements at once;

but before Washington could agree, the Rangers arrived back at the American camp, where word spread quickly through the ranks of Knowlton's stand against the light infantry.[39]

The army's commander recounted his actions to this point to President Hancock: "About the time of the posts departure with my Letter,"—Washington was writing two days after the battle and referred to the correspondence he had sent Hancock on the morning of September 16—"the Enemy appeared in several large bodies upon the plains about Two & a half miles from hence. I rode down to our advanced posts to put matters in a proper situation if they should attempt to come on. When I arrived there, I heard a firing which I was informed was between a party of our Rangers under the Command of Lieutt Col. Knolton, and an advanced party of the Enemy. Our Men came in & told me that the body of the Enemy, who kept themselves concealed consisted of about three Hundred as near as they could guess."[40]

The British were soon close enough that Washington could hear their bugle calls. Various accounts suggest that the buglers were not directing their troops to advance or deploy but were playing "Gone Away," the tune sounded when a fox was killed and the chase over in a hunt.[41] If so, it is uncertain whether the call was meant to mock the retreating Continentals or as an affront to General Washington, known to engage in foxhunts at Mount Vernon.

The evidence appears inconclusive regarding whether any British regimental musicians commonly beat or played signals during military actions in America, although they sometimes played music to intimidate the enemy.[42] Joseph Reed insisted that after the Rangers had been compelled to retreat by a larger force, "the Enemy appeared in open view & in the most insulting manner sounded their Bugle Horns as is usual after a Fox Chase. I never felt such a sensation before, it seem'd to crown our Disgrace."[43] According to one account, the British claimed a different rationale for the bugle call, and that was not to humiliate the rebels but rather to signal that Washington himself had been sighted. His success in eluding capture by His Majesty's forces to that point had allegedly earned him the nickname "The Fox," and so when he was spotted a short distance behind Colonel Reed but out of Reed's sight, one British bugler—in lieu of sounding the regulation "Charge!" on his hunting horn—sounded "Tally Ho!," the traditional signal for a fox sighting.[44]

WASHINGTON'S PLAN

To Colonel Reed, the bugler's call was literally a resounding affront, and he urged his commanding general to respond; however, Washington had to weigh competing considerations. Should he risk precipitating a larger and more perilous engagement without knowing how much support the British were prepared to give Leslie's two light infantry battalions, but knowing that the Black Watch had moved forward to reinforce the latter? On the other hand, would backing down from what the Americans perceived as a blatant insult adversely impact the morale of an army already despondent from its setbacks at Long Island and Kip's Bay? The general resolved this dilemma by devising a scheme designed to entrap at least some of Leslie's men without attempting to drive them back to their lines or otherwise spark a major encounter.

Once Washington determined that the enemy force opposite him on Claremont was not substantial, he proposed an action that would—as he advised Patrick Henry, then serving as Virginia's first post-independence governor—inspire his soldiers in the wake of their recent defeats: "the troops having become in some measure dispirited by these successive retreats, & which I presume has also been the case among several of our Friends in the Country—In order to recover that military Ardor which is of the utmost moment to an Army, almost immediately on my arrival at this place, I formed a design of cutting off some of the Enemy's light troops (who encouraged by their Successes) had advanced to the extremity of the High Ground, opposite to our present incampment."[45]

Washington's "design" was to entice the light infantry on Claremont to descend into the Hollow Way by creating a feint directly in front of them while dispatching a formidable detachment eastward, screened by the terrain and woods, to outflank Leslie's men on their right and hit them in the rear. Although a modest plan, it entailed a degree of coordination and precision in combat that the rebel army had not yet displayed. Washington ordered General John Nixon's brigade—positioned on the extreme right of Greene's division nearest the Hudson River—to deploy 150 volunteers for the frontal demonstration, and Nixon designated Lieutenant Colonel Archibald Crary of Rhode Island to lead them. They were instructed to draw the enemy's attention by making a conspicuous descent into the Hollow Way and creating the impression that they were about to charge up Claremont. Meanwhile, a party of about 230 men commanded by Colonel Knowlton—comprising the Rangers and three companies of riflemen from Colonel George Weedon's 3rd Virginia Regiment—was to execute the flanking maneuver. Major Andrew Leitch led the Virginia contingent that accompanied the Rangers, its three companies commanded by Captains John Ashby, John Thornton, and Charles West, respectively. The 3rd Virginia was a favorite of Washington's as he was familiar with many of its officers from the Fredericksburg area.[46]

Colonel Crary's volunteers came down the slope from the Harlem bluffs through the trees and headed toward Martje David's Fly, a swampy salt marsh by a shallow cove where the Hollow Way met the Hudson River. (This area, which ran along today's 130th Street, was subsequently known as "Harlem Cove" and was later filled in.) They pushed forward until reaching solid ground east of the marsh and at the bottom of the valley where there were several houses with outbuildings and fences. Watching Crary's advance, some of the light infantry took the bait as they moved partway down Claremont to a position behind one of the fences and a hedgerow. Both sides exchanged fire at a distance where it was unlikely anyone would be hit, and then Crary's detachment fell back a few hundred yards seeking to lure the light infantry northward. The redcoats began to move up, and the balance of Nixon's brigade—some eight hundred men—came down the bluffs to reinforce Crary and thereby deter Leslie's troops from advancing too far. A steady firefight ensued between the two forces as they each blazed away at a safe distance, about two hundred yards apart. The Americans had a numerical advantage but were not looking to advance. Neither could their outnumbered adversary.

In a letter to friends, Captain John Chilton, who was with that portion of the 3rd Virginia Regiment stationed on the bluffs, described the frontal feint up to the point where Knowlton's flanking party joined the action: "We discovered the enemy peeping from their heights [on Claremont] over the fencings and rocks and running backwards and forwards. We did not alter our position. I believe they expected we should have ascended the hill to them, but finding us still, they imputed it to fear and came down skipping towards us in small parties." At a distance of about 250 to 300 yards, the redcoats opened fire. According to the captain, "Our orders were not to fire till they came near, but a young officer (of whom we have too many) on the right fired, and it was taken [up] from right to left. We made about four fires. I had fired twice and loaded again, determined to keep for a better chance, but Colonel Weedon calling to keep up our fire (he meant for us to reserve it, but we misunderstood him), I fired once more." Chilton continued: "We then all wiped and loaded and sat down in our ranks and let the enemy fire on us near an hour. Our men observed the best order, not quitting their ranks, though exposed to a constant and warm fire. I can't say enough in their praise; they behaved like soldiers who fought from principle alone." Concurrently, as he noted, "three companies of riflemen from our regiment . . . with other companies of riflemen were flanking the enemy and had began a brisk fire on the right of them."[47]

THE FLANKING MOVEMENT

At about eleven a.m., Knowlton's force set out from Point of Rocks (at today's 127th Street and St. Nicholas Avenue), far east of the fighting, to begin its encircling maneuver. They were accompanied by Colonel Reed, who explained to his wife that "as I had been upon the Ground which no one else had it fell to me to conduct them."[48] Proceeding as unobtrusively as possible, the

Rangers and Virginians crossed the Hollow Way and headed for a rocky rise in an area now encompassed by 123rd and 124th Streets, Broadway, and Amsterdam Avenue, from where they intended to advance south and west to move into position behind the light infantry and seal the trap shut.

By now the fighting just north of Claremont had taken a turn with the presence of Nixon's entire brigade, for the American advantage in firepower forced the outnumbered light infantry to pull back after standing their ground for nearly an hour. In this case, it is possible their success bred failure, as the British retreat may have occurred before Knowlton's men could get in their rear. Nixon's troops headed up the Claremont slope as Leslie's soldiers retired to "a Clear Field about 200 Paces" southwest, "where they lodged themselves behind a Fence covered with Bushes."[49] The detachment led by Knowlton and Leitch may have arrived at the fence at the same time, forcing the light infantry to face the intruders on their right.[50] On the other hand, Joseph Reed attributed the bungled encirclement to a wrong turn, "being unhappily thwarted in my Scheme [to surround the enemy] by some Persons calling to the Troops & taking them out of the Road I intended."[51]

Traditional accounts of the battle suggest that an errant order to fire foiled the American attempt to envelop the light infantry, according to which the culprit was an unidentified officer in the 3rd Virginia Regiment who inexplicably gave the command before the flankers could get behind the enemy—whereupon Knowlton's force began shooting and the British reciprocated.[52] In any case, the planned assault on the British rear was now directed at the right side of their formation instead, and the chance to close the ring was gone.

The exchange of fire between Leslie's men and Knowlton's began just as Major Leitch, positioned at the front of the rebel flankers, reached the top of a ledge on the rocky rise from which they intended to swing southwest behind the enemy. He was struck three times in short order and carried to the rear. "He conducted himself on this occasion in a manner that does him the

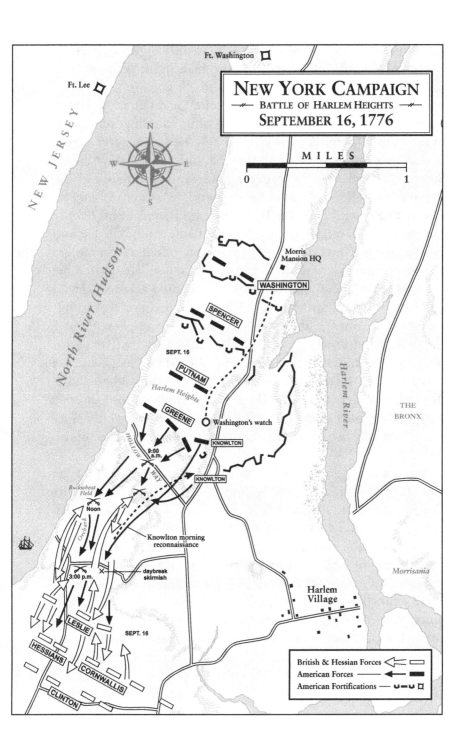

NEW YORK CAMPAIGN
BATTLE OF HARLEM HEIGHTS
SEPTEMBER 16, 1776

greatest Honor and so did all his Party," wrote Colonel David Griffiths of Maryland, "till he received two balls in his belly and one in his hip."[53]

Mounting the same ledge where Leitch had fallen, Knowlton turned to urge his men to follow him while standing in full view of the light infantry. Almost immediately, he was staggered from behind by a British musket ball. Another officer, probably Captain Stephen Brown who succeeded Knowlton in command of the Rangers after the battle, informed a friend, "My poor Colonel . . . was shot just by my Side, the Ball entered the small of his Back—I took hold of him, asked him if he was badly wounded? He told me he was; but, says he, I do not value my Life if we do but get the Day: I then ordered two men to carry him off. He desired me by all Means to keep up this Flank. He seemed as unconcern'd and calm as tho' nothing had happened to him."[54] Another Ranger, Sergeant David Thorp, recalled that "brave commander Colonel [Knowlton] . . . fell within six feet where I was—He begged to be moved so that the enemy should not get possession of his body—I was one who helped put him on the soldiers shoulders who carried him off—He expired in about one hour."[55] Joseph Reed also helped bear Knowlton from the scene: "I assisted him off & when gasping in the Agonies of Death all his Inquiry was if we had drove the enemy."[56]

Historian Margaret MacMillan reminds us that death on the battlefield is frequently sudden and random.[57] Given how notoriously inaccurate muskets were during the Revolution, Knowlton's misfortune may prove the point; however, his habit of leading from the front clearly put him at more than random risk. Perhaps the best-known phrase associated with the colonel was "You cannot lead from behind."[58] Both he and Major Leitch fell while exhorting their men to stand up to the world's finest infantry.[59] In so doing, they were fulfilling the core of the officer code that prevailed in both the American and British armies, which called upon those of high rank to display such manifest bravery as a matter of honor. They obviously did so at their peril.[60] Sir William Howe exemplified the demeanor expected of an eighteenth-century officer when he promised his men before the Battle of Bunker Hill that he would not ask one of them "to go a step further than where I go myself at your head."[61] (He was true to his word but emerged with only a slight injury to his foot whereas every member of his staff was killed or wounded.) According to historian Charles Royster, American officers self-consciously adopted a long-standing conviction among European armies that an officer's honor was a mark of distinction reflecting "a gentleman's conspicuous superiority," which earned him the common soldier's deference and thereby enabled him to exercise command.[62]

When reporting on the September 16 engagement to Patrick Henry, Washington would weigh the gains and losses from implementing his plan to outflank the light infantry: "To effect this salutary purpose Colo. Knolton & Majr Leitch were detached with parties of Riflemen and rangers to get in their rear, while a disposition was made as if to attack them in front—By some unhappy mistake the fire was commenced from that quarter, rather on their flank than in the Rear, by which means though the Enemy were defeated & pushed off the Ground, yet they had an opportunity of retreating to their Main Body—This piece of success (though it tended greatly to inspire our troops with confidence) has been in some measure imbittered by the loss of those two brave Officers, who are dead of the Wounds they received in the Action."[63]

THE ACTION WIDENS

Despite losing Knowlton and Leitch, the Rangers and Virginians continued to trade fire with the light infantry positioned behind the bush-covered fence. This was quite possibly the pivotal moment in the battle, when the fall of the two officers in command of the flanking contingent—one right after the other—might have so dispirited their men as to enfeeble their attack. Indeed, they might have broken apart in confusion.[64] That they stood their ground is a tribute to the resolve and competence of the officers and men in the detachment. Perhaps they fought all the harder to avenge the loss of their commanding officers.[65] Captain

Brown of the Rangers, along with Captains Ashby, Thornton, and West leading the three companies pulled from the Virginia 3rd Regiment, managed their men ably and continued to press hard against the enemy right. Simultaneously, Colonel Crary's force in the British front, which had pushed the light infantry back to the fence after being reinforced by the entirety of Nixon's brigade, began to escalate their attack. Observing from atop the bluffs, Washington ordered in additional reinforcements from Greene's division to support Crary's troops. These included nine companies from General Beall's Maryland militia, Colonel Sargent's entire Massachusetts brigade, and Colonel Douglas's 5th Connecticut State Levies who were looking to atone for their dismal performance at Kip's Bay the day before.

Washington related to John Hancock the maneuvers that occurred after Knowlton and Leitch were wounded: "Their Men however persevered & continued the Engagement with the greatest resolution. Finding that they wanted a support, I advanced part of Colo. [David] Griffiths and Colo. [William] Richardson's Maryland Regiments with some detachments from the Eastern Regiments who were nearest the place of Action. These Troops charged the Enemy with great Intrepidity and drove them from the Wood into the plain, and were pushing them from thence, (having silenced their fire in a great measure)."[66]

At this point, the light infantry posted behind the fence were clearly overmatched. Although heavily outnumbered, they had stubbornly resisted the assault in front and on their right but now were forced to give way in the face of superior firepower. Their overconfidence had lured them into a trap, which they would be fortunate to escape but only because of the aborted rebel effort at encirclement; however, Leslie's men fought well, as one would have expected given their proud and long-standing tradition of service. They had crossed an ocean to fight a war that some historians opine was unwinnable, or at least would be after General Howe's failure to destroy the Continental Army in 1776 (and even more so after France entered the contest in 1778). Notwithstanding Britain's vaunted naval superiority and its army's advantages in equipment, training, experience, and discipline, the challenges of conquering and holding the vast area encompassed by its thirteen rebellious provinces and doing so at the end of a three-thousand-mile-long supply line were arguably insuperable.[67] In addition, the nature of that domain was especially problematic for the Crown's military designs, as its predominantly hilly and forested terrain was very different from the Low Countries, where most British officers had their formative military experience, and was naturally advantageous to defenders—who were rebel soldiers more often than not.[68]

Most British infantry came from humble backgrounds as farmers, laborers, and tradesmen, and a small number were convicts who opted for military service over incarceration when given the chance. They had volunteered for the army and many made it a career, given the steady employment and pay. Despite its inherent dangers, a soldier's life represented an appealing alternative to working-class youth in Britain who otherwise faced the prospect of long hours of wearisome and sometimes hazardous manual labor or an apprenticeship under exploitative conditions in which they could be overworked or beaten without recourse.[69] Many of His Majesty's troops believed their unit was the best in the army and were encouraged to do so. They were also intensely loyal to the monarchy and in that respect stood in firm opposition to those supporting the American rebellion.[70] The British regulars were motivated by certain ideals as important to them as the cause of liberty was to their American counterparts, for to them this conflict was not primarily about power or interest but rather these values to which they were deeply committed—discipline, duty, fidelity, honor, loyalty, and service.[71]

Committed or not, Leslie's men were on the verge of being overwhelmed by a larger force as morning turned to afternoon on September 16. They were compelled to retreat from their position behind the fence, firing at their pursuers as they withdrew. Instead of retracing their steps back up the slope of Claremont, however, the redcoats fell back through the woods along a line that paralleled today's Broadway and up a much less steep hill, taking the shortest route back toward their main encampment. The sight of these scarlet-clothed warriors giving ground was a new one for the rebel attackers, and they relished the moment.[72] At the top of the slope lay a large open field of buckwheat that ran across the entire crest, extending south from today's 120th Street to almost 116th Street and from Riverside Drive east to about Broadway. Part of this property was owned by Adrian Hoaglandt and the rest by Harman Vandewater.

With the Americans close on their heels, the light infantry, now in urgent need of reinforcements, made a stand along the northern rim of the buckwheat field. General Leslie had called in the remaining soldiers of the 2nd and 3rd light infantry battalions and the Black Watch, in addition to which elements of General Cornwallis's Corps de Reserve were moving up toward the fighting. These included a Hessian rifle company, a pair of small field guns, the grenadiers of the 33rd Regiment of Foot, and the battalion of Hessian grenadiers commanded by Lieutenant Colonel Otto von Linsing from Colonel von Donop's brigade. If all the reinforcements had joined the battle, more than five thousand soldiers would have been deployed against the rebels.[73]

By noon, the number of soldiers involved in the fighting had grown far beyond what Washington had contemplated. The opposing formations were still relatively small, but this had become a real battle with two formal lines pitted against each other. Perhaps as many as two thousand rebel soldiers were positioned in the buckwheat field at the top of the hill, with Generals Putnam, Greene, and George Clinton—an American cousin of British General Henry Clinton—as well as Colonel Reed, all present at this stage of the contest. Nixon's brigade formed the right of the American line; Sargent's brigade, Beall's militia, and Douglas's Connecticut State Levies occupied the center; and the Rangers, Weedon's 3rd Virginia Regiment, and Griffiths's and Richardson's Maryland Regiments were posted on the left. The bulk of the American forces engaged were from New England (Connecticut, Massachusetts, and Rhode Island), Maryland, and Virginia.[74] The American line ran just north of today's 120th Street with the

British extended along 119th Street or just south of it, the area in between a virtual no-man's land.[75]

Although the redcoats were outnumbered, their line stood firm for some time as the units involved were among the best in Howe's army.[76] They were greatly helped by two brass 3-pounders maneuvered into the buckwheat field from McGowan's Way by gun crews under Lieutenant Wallace of the Royal Artillery. The crews fired sixty rounds from each piece, exhausting the ammunition supply they had brought with them.

Meanwhile, Generals Greene, Putnam, and George Clinton, together with Colonel Reed and several of Washington's aides, rode back and forth behind the American line calling out words of encouragement to their men, no doubt inspired by what they were seeing—a firmness of purpose unlike any the Patriot army had generally exhibited until now.[77] A journal entry by Lieutenant David Dimock of Connecticut recorded his emotions in the throes of combat: "I could not help feeling an involuntary tremor, as though my knees were giving away, as I was obliged to stand still and listen to the steady 'tramp, tramp' of the approaching foe, but as soon as we received their fire and the man at my right-hand side fell forward shot through the heart, the blood spouting in a stream from his bosom, at the sight of that blood all the tremor was gone in an instant, and vengeance was the only feeling."[78]

There were exceptions to this display of fortitude, however, as Joseph Reed explained when he recounted to his wife the perils he faced on this occasion, both from enemy fire and his own side. The latter ensued from his encounter with a reluctant warrior, Private Ebenezer Leffingwell, who sought to escape the scene: "You will probably hear from other Quarters the double Escape I had—My own Horse not being at Hand I borrowed one from a young Philadelphian—he received a Shot just behind his fore Shoulder which narrowly missed my Leg. I am told that he is since dead—But the greatest was from one of our own Rascals who was running away, upon my driving him back a second Time he presented his Piece & snapp'd at me at about a Rod Distance—I seized a Piece from another Soldier & snapp'd at him—but he had the same good Luck. He has been since tried & is now under Sentence of Death—but I believe I must beg him off as after I found I could not get the Gun off, I wounded him in the Head & cut off his thumb with my Hanger." Leffingwell was court-martialed and sentenced to death a week after the battle, but Reed interceded on his behalf at the last moment to spare him.[79]

Leffingwell aside, the rebel units present—including Douglas's green 5th Connecticut State Levies who had fled from the invaders at Kip's Bay—exhibited a remarkable lift in spirits from their nadir following the previous day's events.[80] Notwithstanding this, Colonel Reed offered an unverifiable and somewhat self-congratulatory observation about their performance: "I suppose many Persons will think it was rash & imprudent for Officers of our Rank to go into such an action (Gen' Puttnam, Gen. Green, many of the General's family—M' Tilghman [Captain Tench Tilghman, Washington's aide-de-camp] &c were in it) but it was really done to animate the Troops who were quite dispirited & would not go into Danger unless their officers led the Way."[81]

THE BRITISH GIVE WAY

The clash at the buckwheat field continued for almost two hours until the British began to fall back. Lieutenant Wallace's two-gun battery had almost run out of ammunition, and Leslie's men were low on theirs. They had eschewed their favorite tactic, the bayonet charge, and at about two p.m. Captain Tilghman reported to Washington, observing from the bluffs, that the light infantry were slowly withdrawing. Anticipating the arrival of additional reinforcements on the other side, the commander-in-chief thought it best not to advance beyond the buckwheat field and risk precipitating a general action. He instructed Tilghman to convey orders to the officers in charge for the Americans to disengage and pull back. The decision was a timely one for, in fact, Anglo-German reinforcements—Cornwallis's reserves and the Linsing battalion of Hessian grenadiers—were approaching the buckwheat field after a forced march of about three miles.[82] As Washington explained to John Hancock, "I judged It prudent to order a Retreat, fearing the Enemy (as I have since found was really the case) were sending a large Body to support their party."[83]

Before Tilghman could return to the battlefield with Washington's orders, however, the British had begun to retreat through the orchards below the buckwheat field and across the Bloomingdale Road. In so doing, they retraced their steps over the ground on which they had pursued Knowlton's Rangers that morning, and then headed southward toward Striker's Bay on the west side of the island at about today's Ninety-sixth Street, to seek protective cover from the guns of the British frigates anchored there. Some of the rebel soldiers chased after them without waiting for orders, animated by the spectacle of their adversary in flight, and sporadic skirmishing flared briefly—at what is now 111th Street and even farther south, almost to Nicholas Jones's farmhouse at today's 106th Street. When the warships at Striker's Bay opened fire on the pursuing Americans, the latter apparently lost their enthusiasm for the chase. Although too far away and too high above the Hudson to be within reach of those shells, they halted their advance and returned to their lines. By then Tilghman had delivered Washington's orders, and the Patriot combatants commenced an orderly march back to their camp on Harlem Heights.[84]

PARTICIPANT ACCOUNTS

In a letter to his father three days after the clash initiated by Knowlton's Rangers, Captain Tilghman outlined the flow of battle as it had unfolded: "On Monday last we had a pretty sharp Skirmish with the British Troops which was brought on in the following Manner. The General rode down to our farthest Lines, and when he came near them heard a firing which he was informed was between our Scouts and the out Guards of the Enemy. When our men came in they informed the General that there were a party of about 300 behind a woody hill, tho' they only showed a very small party to us."

The captain explained that Washington "laid a plan for attacking them in the Rear and cutting off their Retreat which was to be effected in the following Manner. Major Leitch with three companies of Col. Weedons Virginia Regiment, and Col. Knowlton with his Rangers were to steal round while a party were to march towards them and seem as if they intended to attack in front, but not to make any real Attack till they saw our Men fairly in their Rear. The Bait took as to one part, as soon as they saw our party in front the Enemy ran down the Hill and took possession of some Fences and Bushes and began to fire at them, but at too great distance to do much execution."

As Tilghman noted, Washington's plan to envelop the enemy force was doomed by the precipitous assault on Leslie's right: "Unluckily Col. Knowlton and Major Leitch began their Attack too soon, it was rather in Flank than in Rear. The Action now grew warm, Major Leitch was wounded early in the Engagement and Col. Knowlton soon after, the latter mortally." At this point, Washington "ordered over part of Col. Griffiths's and part of Col. Richardson's Maryland Regiments, these Troops tho' young charged with as much Bravery as I can conceive, they gave two fires and then rushed right forward which drove the Enemy from the Wood into a Buckwheat field, from whence they retreated. The General fearing (as we afterwards found) that a large Body was coming up to support them, sent me over to bring our Men off. They gave a Hurra and left the Field in good Order."

According to Tilghman, the opposing force "was much more considerable than we imagined when the General ordered the Attack. It consisted of the 2d. Battn. of light Infantry, a Battn. of the Royal Highlanders and 3 Comps. of Hessian Rifle Men. The prisoners we took, told us, they expected our Men would have run away as they did the day before, but that they were never more surprised than to see us advancing to attack them."[85]

Writing to the New York Convention on September 18, General George Clinton observed, "I consider our Success in this small affair, at this Time, almost equal to a Victory. It has animated our troops, gave them new Spirits, and erazed every bad impression, the retreat from Long Island, &c. had left on their minds, they find they are able, with inferior Numbers, to drive their Enemy, and think of nothing the outcome in this encounter now but Conquest."[86] Clinton's observation overlooks the fact that the American forces outnumbered the enemy troops who were engaged during most of the fighting on September 16. In a letter to Dr. Peter Tappen three days later, he described how the battle played out once the British were pushed back from Martje David's Fly and took post behind the bush-covered fence: "our People pursued them but being oblidged to stand exposed in the open Field or take a Fence at a Considerable Distance they preferred the Latter it was indeed adviseable for we soon brought a Couple of Field Pieces to bear upon them which fairly put them to flight with two Discharges only the Second Time our People pursued them closely to the Top of a Hill about 400 paces distant where they received a very Considerable Reinforcement & made their Second Stand Our People also had received a Considerable Reinforcement." This was the buckwheat field, and "at this Place a very brisk Action commenced which continued for near two Hours in which Time we drove the Enemy into a Neighbouring orchard from that across a Hollow & up another Hill not far Distant from their own Encampment." There, this narrative concluded, "we found the Ground rather Disadvantageous & a Retreat insecure we therefore thot proper not to pursue them any farther & retired to our first Ground leaving the Enemy on the last Ground we drove them to."[87]

On the British side, the accounts of various officers, although perhaps self-serving in some instances, bear witness to their efforts in the face of an unexpected turn of events—an unprecedented assault by the rebel army. Captain George Harris recalled how his grenadiers came to the assistance of Leslie's light infantry: "The 16th of September we were ordered to stand to our arms at eleven a.m. and were instantly trotted about three miles (without a halt to draw breath), to support a battalion of light infantry, which had imprudently advanced so far without support as to be in great danger of being cut off. This must have happened, but for our haste. So dangerous a quality is courage without prudence for its guide; with it, how noble and respectable it makes the man."[88]

Captain John Montresor, an engineer and aide to General

Howe, brought up the two field pieces in Lieutenant Wallace's two-gun battery to fend off the American attack, as he explained in his journal: "The 16th Sept., 1776, the action on Vandewater's Height, near Harlaem, on New York Island, I procured two 3 Pounders, Brass, with Lt: Wallace, Royal Artillery. No horses being near McGowns's, where the Guns were, had them hauled by hand, and brought into action to face the Enemy, who were attempting to cut off our Left, and getting round us between our Left and Hudson's River. The proposal was my own, and had its desired effect, no other Guns being in the Field, and 60 rounds from each were fired."[89]

Loftus Cliffe, an Irish-born lieutenant with the 46th Regiment, wrote admiringly of its light infantry company's adroit performance under Captain Mathew Johnson's unorthodox direction: "Johnson and his Company behaved amazingly, he goes thro his manavers by a whistle for which he has often been laughed at, they either form to right or left or squat or rise by a particular whistle which his men are as well acquainted with as the Battalion with the word of Command, he being used to Woods fighting and having a quick Eye had his Company down in the Moment of the Enemies present & up again at the advantageous moment for their fire, killed several and had not one of his Company hurt during the whole time he drove the Enemy before him." According to Cliffe, Johnson "upon the retreat tho' managed in the coolest manner he had Seven Wounded, not one of whom would suffer themselves to be taken precipitously off and some continued their fire after being severely wounded."[90]

Hessian Colonel Carl von Donop, commander of the Jäger Corps, reported to his superior, General Leopold von Heister, "But for my Yagers [Jägers], two Regiments of Highlanders and the British infantry would have all, perhaps, been captured, for they were attacked by a force four times their number; and Gen. Leslie had made a great blunder in sending these brave fellows so far in advance in the woods without support."[91] Major C. L. Baurmeister echoed Donop's report, while exaggerating the number of their adversary engaged: "The English Light Infantry advanced too quickly on the retreat of the enemy and . . . fell into an ambuscade of four thousand men, and if the Grenadiers and especially the Hessian Yagers had not arrived in time to help them no one of these brave Light Infantry would have escaped."[92]

ASSESSING THE OUTCOME

George Washington realized at once how welcome the events of September 16 were to his hard-pressed soldiery. The next day, he issued the following congratulatory order to the army: "The General most heartily thanks the Troops commanded yesterday by Major Leitch, who first advanced on the Enemy and the others who so resolutely supported them; the Behaviour Yesterday is such a Contrast to that of some Troops the day before, as must shew what may be done where Officers and Soldiers will exert themselves. Once more therefore the General calls upon Officers and Men to act up to the Noble Cause in which they are engaged, and support the Honour and Liberties of their Country." It seems curious that Washington mentioned Leitch and not Knowlton here, considering that he referenced both in a similar context in other correspondence about the battle, for example, in his letter to John Hancock on September 18 and the New York State Convention on September 23. It should also be noted that Washington, in the congratulatory order to the army on September 17, paid tribute to the "Gallant and brave Col. Knowlton" in the paragraph immediately following the one quoted above, which is cited elsewhere in this chapter. Perhaps the commander-in-chief's mention of Major Leitch in the order, before his reference to Knowlton, reflected an underlying affinity for a fellow Virginian, but it would not appear to evince any lessening of his regard for the colonel.[93]

Clearly the Crown's forces "met with a very different kind of Reception from what they did the day before," observed Nathanael Greene, who had experienced his first taste of battle.[94] He noted that His Majesty's soldiers, "flushed with the successes of the day before, approached and attacked our Lines, which I had the Honor to Command. The Action or rather Skirmish lasted about two hours; our people beat the enemy off the ground."[95] Colonel Weedon of the 3rd Virginia Regiment encapsulated the outcome of this encounter for their foe: "Upon the whole they got cursedly thrashed."[96]

Certainly nothing in General Howe's account of the battle as conveyed to Lord George Germain—which inflated the number of Americans involved—suggested that his side had been treated so rudely: "On the 16th in the morning a large party of the enemy having passed under cover of the woods near to the advanced posts of the army by way of Vanderwater's Height, the 2d and 3d battalions of light infantry, supported by the 42nd regiment pushed forward, and drove them back to their entrenchments, from whence the enemy observing they were not in force, attacked them with near 3000 men, which occasioned the march of the reserve with two field pieces, a battalion of Hessian grenadiers and a company of chasseurs, to prevent the corps engaged from being surrounded." Howe assured Germain that "the light infantry and 42nd regiment with the assistance of the chasseurs and field pieces repulsed the enemy with considerable loss, and obliged them to retire within their works."[97] Even so, at least one of his officers conceded that the rebels had performed admirably. Lieutenant Cliffe of the 46th Regiment opined that if this affair "was a scheme of Washington's, it certainly was well-concerted."[98]

Connecticut's Captain David Humphreys recounted that the Patriot soldiers who fought on this day, to a man, "behaved with the greatest intrepidity. So bravely did they repulse the British, that Sir William Howe moved his *reserve*, with two field-pieces, a battalion of Hessian grenadiers, and a company of chasseurs, to succor his retreating troops. General Washington not willing to draw on a general action, declined pressing the pursuit. In this engagement were the second and third battalions of light infantry, the forty-second British regiment, and the German Chasseurs, of whom eight officers, and upward of seventy privates were wounded, and our people buried nearly twenty, who were left dead on the field. We had about forty wounded; our loss in killed, except of two valuable officers, was very inconsiderable."

Humphreys affirmed the Americans' boost in morale from this relatively small battle: "An advantage so trivial in itself produced, in event, a surprising and almost incredible effect upon the whole army. Amongst the troops not engaged, who, during the action, were throwing earth from the new trenches, with an alacrity that indicated a determination to defend them, every visage was seen to brighten, and to assume, instead of the gloom of despair, the glow of animation. This change, no less sudden than happy, left little room to doubt that the men, who ran the day before at the sight of an enemy, would now, to wipe away the stain of that disgrace, and to recover the confidence of their general, have conducted themselves in a very different manner."[99]

In a letter written on September 18, Maryland's Colonel David Griffiths observed that "our troops behaved in a manner that does them the highest Honor. After keeping a heavy fire on both sides for near three hours they drove the enemy to their main Body and then were prudently ordered to retreat for fear of being drawn into an ambuscade. . . . This affair, tho' not great in itself, is of consequence as it gives spirits to the army, which they wanted. Indeed the confusion was such on Sunday [September 15] that everybody looked dispirited. At present everything wears a different face."[100]

Private Joseph Plumb Martin, who claimed to have met his fellow Connecticut resident Thomas Knowlton years before, recorded his impression of the battle and particularly the actions of "our rangers and some few other light troops, under the command of Colonel Knowlton, and Major Leitch of (I believe) Virginia." He recalled that "Colonel Knowlton, a brave man, and commander of the detachment, fell in the early part of the engagement. It was said, by those who saw it, that he lost his valuable life by unadvisedly exposing himself singly to the enemy. In my boyhood I had been acquainted with him; he was a brave man and an excellent citizen." With Knowlton and Leitch having fallen, "the troops, who were then engaged, were left with no higher commanders than their captains, but they still kept the enemy retreating."[101] When the fighting ceased, the condition of the exhausted and hungry defenders was such that they could barely savor the moment. Martin reported, "We remained on the battle ground till nearly sunset, expecting the enemy to attack us again, but they showed no such inclination that day. The men were very much fatigued and faint, having had nothing to eat for forty-eight hours,—at least the greater part were in this condition, and I among the rest."[102]

KILLED AND WOUNDED

To put American casualties in this battle into comparative perspective, by Henry P. Johnston's account they exceeded those at Bennington, Vermont (August 16, 1777); Stony Point, New York (July 16, 1779); and King's Mountain (October 7, 1780) and Cowpens (January 17, 1781) in South Carolina—all American victories, with the last two ranking among the most one-sided engagements of the war. According to Johnston's estimate, the nearly 1,800 rebel troops engaged at Harlem Heights were slightly less in number than those at Bennington but larger than those in the other three encounters.[103]

Casualty counts on both sides are imprecise.[104] British and Hessian losses may have run as high as ninety killed and three hundred wounded, as compared with American casualties of thirty dead and less than one hundred wounded; but among the rebel fallen were four officers, including two exceptional ones in Knowlton and Leitch—a severe jolt to the Continental Army.[105] Add to them Captain Micaijah Gleason of Nixon's Massachusetts Regiment and Lieutenant Noell Allen of Varnum's Rhode Island Regiment, and in that respect the American loss exceeded the enemy's.[106]

Benjamin Trumbull of the Connecticut militia noted that "few men were Killed and wounded on the side of the Provincials considering the Heat and duration of the Action. . . . [but it] appeared by the blood and trails of the Enemy where they retreated that their Loss was considerable."[107] Colonel Gold Silliman, also with the Connecticut militia, told his wife: "Our loss on this occasion by the best information is about 25 killed & 40 or 50 wounded. The enemy by the best accounts have suffered much more than we. . . . They have found now that when we meet them on equal ground we are not a set of people that will run from them—but that they have now had a pretty good drubbing, tho' this was an action between but a small part of the army."[108] According to General George Clinton, American casualties included, besides Knowlton and Leitch, sixteen privates killed and between eight and ten subalterns and privates wounded, but he was uncertain as to the extent of the enemy's loss: "They carried their Dead and wounded off, in and soon after the Action; but we have good Evidence of their having upwards of 60 kill'd, & violent presumption of 100."[109] Captain Tench Tilghman, Washington's aide, observed that "We had about 40 wounded and a very few killed. A [British] Serjeant who deserted says their Accounts were 89 wounded and 8 killed, but in the latter he is mistaken for we have buried more than double that Number."[110]

Captain Samuel Richards of Connecticut recalled his experience overseeing the interment of the fallen on both sides: "The next day I had a mournful duty assigned to me—the command of a covering party over the fatigue men who buried the dead who fell in the action the previous day. I placed myself and party on a small eminence so as to see the men at their work, and to discover the enemy should they approach to interrupt them. There was 32 or 33 bodies found on the field, and were drawn to a large hole which was prepared for the purpose and buried together. One body of a fine limbed young man had been brought into the camp with a bullet hole in the breast near the region of the heart." The sight of this grisly labor compelled Richards to reflect "on the force of habit: to see those fatigue men performing this duty with as little concern as they would have performed any common duty."[111]

Most British estimates significantly undercounted their losses. The tally of Stephen Kemble, deputy adjutant general to William Howe and a New Jersey native, reflected those calculations: "1 Serjeant and 13 Privates Killed; 2 Majors, 2 Captains, 7 Subaltens, 5 Serjeants, 3 Drummers, and 138 Wounded."[112] In his report to George Germain, General Howe understated his casualties and overstated those of the rebels, consistent with his penchant for doing so, while alluding to the deaths of Knowlton and Leitch: "The enemy's loss is not ascertained; but from the accounts of deserters it is agreed, that they had not less than 300 killed and wounded, among them a colonel and a major killed. We had eight officers wounded most of them very slightly; fourteen men killed and about 70 wounded."[113]

Hessian Major C. L. Baurmeister insisted there were heavy losses on both sides. He claimed the light infantry had "lost 70 dead and 200 wounded" but that "the enemy must have lost very severely, because no Yager had any ammunition left, and all the Highlanders had fired their last shot. A lieutenant of the Yagers, Henrichs, was wounded in the left side and also four Yagers."[114]

Captain George Harris of the 5th Regiment's grenadiers commented on the disparities he had witnessed between the appearance of injury and the severity of a wound: "A man in my company had his hat shot through nearly in the direction of my wound, but the ball merely raised the skin; and in the battalion on our left a man was shot so dead when lying on the ground, that the next man did not perceive it, but when he got up to stand to his arms, kicked his comrade, thinking he was asleep, and then found, to his great surprise, that he was quite dead, a ball having entered under the ear, and very little blood having issued from it."

In a more light-hearted vein, the captain recounted how his sustenance was impacted by the day's events: "Before we started in the morning, our dinner, consisting of a goose and piece of mutton, had been put on the fire. The moment we marched, our domestic deposited the above named delicacies on a chaise, and followed us with it to our ground. When the fight was over, he again hung the goose to the fire, but the poor bird had been scarcely half done, when we were ordered to return to our station. There again we commenced cooking, and though without dish, plate, or knife did ample justice to our fare, which we washed down with bad rum and water."[115]

Hessian Lieutenant John Heinrichs, who was wounded in the battle, described his injury and his good fortune in being able to seek assistance from one of the families of means whose houses he had liberated from rebel control after landing at Kip's Bay on the 15th. According to the lieutenant, these families, who had fled "and left their slaves behind" along with their "furniture, rural riches, and jewels," shed "joyful tears of gratitude" when learning, upon their return, that he had "delivered their property back to their hands." The next day, Heinrichs "at one o'clock . . . was compelled to withdraw" from the fighting, "as I was shot by a rifle-ball in the left side of the breast 4 fingers distant from the heart. To whom could I more safely go, and who would receive me in a more friendly manner than they who had but yesterday called me their benefactor, their preserver?" The wounded officer sought a quiet setting: "As I do not like noise, now still less than ever; I selected for myself, although I could have chosen palaces, a small house on the East River, to which the widow of a New York preacher, Oglyby, had fled with a numerous family of children and step-children. . . . All these people came back last evening; and the emotion I felt on seeing mother and children, grandfather and grandchildren, &c. down to the black children of the slaves, hugging and kissing each other, so affected my wound, that I got a fever in the night. Not to be thought of are the flatteries the good people showered on me which I did not deserve, as I acted only according to orders."[116]

The outcome for soldiers on either side who were wounded in this and other Revolutionary War engagements was often fatal and frequently horrific. For many a brave combatant, death in the field was more merciful than the suffering he would endure if wounded. There were never enough surgeons to meet the need, and the ones available were often crude, incompetent, and lacking adequate supplies or knowledge. Many wounded were left to die where they fell, especially if the army was on the move, and the unfortunate ones who made it to the hospital lay on the ground or on wooden benches awaiting their turn with a surgeon who commonly relied on amputation or some primitive treatment. The wounded and dying were packed together with men suffering from all forms of disease.[117] American soldiers typically regarded the hospital as a place to be avoided at any cost, and many, if they had been in one, could say nothing good about their experience.[118] The suffering of the wounded, who were left without any means of easing pain or healing infections, reflected the primitive state of eighteenth-century medicine. Mortality from amputations of the upper leg was between 60 and 80 percent and from hip wounds exceeded 90 percent, while abdominal wounds almost always resulted in death. In short, for many there was no hope of recovery.[119]

LEADERSHIP

George Washington's aggressive military instincts had been aroused by the British advance against his lines on the morning of September 16, coming as it did so soon after what he viewed as a disgraceful failure to mount any effective resistance to the landing at Kip's Bay. The general was looking for a fight as he was temperamentally disposed to do throughout the conflict, even at risk to his army. In that respect, he exhibited an eagerness for battle at variance with an impression—suggested in some of his writing and in various quarters—that he sought to wage a defensive war.[120] In all likelihood, Washington's willingness to engage with the enemy on the 16th would have proven exceedingly short-sighted if the fighting had drawn in a much larger portion of the British and Hessian forces stationed south of where the action occurred. "This skirmish might have brought on a general action," according to General Heath, "for both armies were then within supporting distance of the troops which were engaged."[121] Fortunately for the commander-in-chief and his soldiers, that was not the case and he had the good sense not to push his luck too far.

In fact, the British command had no plans to engage the Americans on this day or in the immediate future, contrary to what Washington may have thought.[122] General Howe no more wanted to assault a fortified position on Harlem Heights in September than he had on Brooklyn Heights in August. Instead, he busied himself establishing his new headquarters in lower Manhattan and basking in the welcome extended by many residents who regarded the redcoats as liberators.[123] Howe's orders of September 17 commended "the Bravery of the few troops that yesterday beat back a verry superior body of the Rebels" but disapproved the "want of attention in the Light Companies pursuing the Rebels without that proper Discretion to be observed when there is not troops to support."[124]

Henry Clinton faulted the imprudent conduct of Leslie's men in pursuing Knowlton's Rangers to begin with but, reflecting his tense relations with Howe, implied that if the Crown's forces had advanced in force on the 16th and taken Bloomingdale Heights, they would have been poised to ford the Harlem River, outflank the Americans on their left, and gain a position at King's Bridge behind their opponent. This was an objective Clinton had repeatedly endorsed.[125] That morning, he had gone to "take command of the foreposts [and] found that the light infantry, having with rather too much impetuosity pursued some parties of rebels toward their works, had got themselves somewhat disadvantageously engaged under a heavy fire of grape, upon which I directly advised the officer who led them to fall back a few yards to more favorable ground."

While vastly overstating the number of Americans involved, Clinton reported that the British withdrawal "was effected with certain precautions but not without some loss, as the rebels were in considerable force—not less than 7000 men. It, however, appears that we might have held this post, which would have probably been a better one than that we took afterward, as it might have saved us the dangerous passage of Hell Gate." Clinton added, with a hint of sarcasm, that General Howe "had, without doubt, very sufficient reasons for me to retreat, which we did at dusk without receiving a single shot from the enemy."[126]

Stephen Kemble's comments suggest that doubts about the need for the encounter were fairly widespread on the British side: "In the morning a Party of the Enemy showed themselves at Jones's House; were inconsiderately pursued by two Companies of Light Infantry who Engaged and drove a very Superior Body to a great distance, supported by 42d. Regiment and some Light Infantry; were fired at from a Breast work, and, it not being thought proper to support them, were ordered to Retreat."[127] Captain William Evelyn's letter to his aunt on September 24 described the Harlem Heights "skirmish" against the rebels as achieving "no other end than to prove our superiority even in their beloved woods, as the ground we gained we did not want, but went back at night to what we left in the morning."[128]

REMEMBERING THE FALLEN

With his dying words, Thomas Knowlton allegedly urged his eldest son Frederick, then serving with the Rangers and nearing his sixteenth birthday, to fight for his country.[129] The colonel was carried to the Cross Keys Tavern on King's Bridge Road where he expired in the afternoon, while Major Leitch was removed to the Blue Bell Tavern and clung to life there for another two weeks.[130] He breathed his last on October 1 or 2.[131] In death, Frederick's father was lauded by Washington in his General Orders as "the gallant and brave Colonel Knowlton who would have been an honor to any Country"[132] and in a letter to John Hancock as one whose "fall is much to be regretted, as that of a brave & good Officer."[133]

The sentiments expressed by the commander-in-chief were widely shared by other soldiers and those sympathetic to the Revolutionary cause. Joseph Reed, when writing to his wife about the Harlem Heights engagement, observed that "our greatest loss was a brave Officer from Connecticut whose Name & Spirit ought to be immortalized, one Col Knowlton."[134] Captain Tilghman eulogized Knowlton as "one of the bravest and best officers in the army" and praised his Rangers, and the 3rd Virginia Regiment that lost Major Leitch, for having "persisted with the greatest bravery" during the balance of the fighting in spite of their loss.[135] General George Clinton, in relating the events of September 16, referred to Knowlton as "a brave Officer who was killed in the Action."[136] Corresponding with his son Joseph, the Continental Army's commissary general, Governor Trumbull of Connecticut, as ardent a Patriot as there was, echoed the mournful litany: "I lament the loss of the brave Lt. Col. Knowlton—would others behave with the spirit and bravery he did, our affairs would soon put

on a different aspect."[137] And Private Oliver Burnham of Knowlton's Rangers later alluded "to the honor due Colonel Knowlton
and his family for his conduct on that day—He had a brother
[Burnham was referring to Thomas's older brother Daniel, an ensign with the Rangers] and Son in the battle, all brave men."[138]

Knowlton was buried in an unmarked grave along what is now
St. Nicholas Avenue between 135th and 145th streets in New York
City.[139] According to General William Heath, a fellow New Eng-
lander, the colonel's remains "were interred with military hon-
ours" on September 17.[140]

Major Leitch was buried in a swale along the Post Road.[141]
Fourteen years later, his daughter Sarah would write to President
Washington, noting that her father "actuated by Zeal in the cause
of this Country entered into the Army of these States, and in the
year 1776 Sacrificed his Life in executing the orders of his General." On behalf of herself and her brother James, who had lost
their mother shortly after Andrew's death, Sarah did "humbly in-
treat therefore that the half pay of the Commission possessed by
their said Father, may be extended to your Petitioners commenc-
ing from the date of his Death, or for such other provision as you
may think most proper."[142]

The final rites for Knowlton and Leitch, as for those of other
fallen officers, would have mirrored the various distinctions of
rank in the Continental Army. Officers and those who served
under them were buried separately, and the rank and file were
generally interred in a perfunctory manner while the ritual for
officers was marked by ceremony and elaborate formalities.[143]
Moreover, officers who died in battle, unlike the common soldiers
who met a similar end, were paid tribute in general orders, newspapers, and public orations—but then the enlisted man no more
expected equal treatment in death than in life.[144] For as Joseph
Plumb Martin, who never rose above the rank of sergeant, observed from his long soldierly ordeal, "Great men get great praise,
little men nothing. But it always was so and always will be."[145]

Private Martin illustrated the reality of the common soldier's
relative anonymity in his recollection of an incident that followed

the Harlem Heights engagement: "A circumstance occurred on the evening after this action, which although trifling in its nature, excited in me feelings which I shall never forget. When we came off the field we brought away a man who had been shot dead upon the spot; and after we had refreshed ourselves we proceeded to bury him." The grave was dug on the grounds of the Morris house that served as Washington's headquarters, where Martin's party endeavored, "just in the dusk of evening, to commit the poor man, then far from friends and relatives, to the bosom of his mother earth."

As soon as they laid him in the ground, "in as decent a posture as existing circumstances would permit, there came from the house, towards the grave, two young ladies who appeared to be sisters;—as they approached the grave, the soldiers immediately made way for them." When the women reached "the head of the grave, they stopped, and with their arms around each other's neck, stooped forward and looked into it." They "asked if we were going to put the earth upon his naked face," and when "answered in the affirmative, one of them took a fine white gauze handkerchief from her neck" and asked that it be used to cover his face, as "tears, at the same time, [were] flowing down their cheeks." Once the grave was filled, they returned to the house.

Although no one there knew the man being buried, "yet he had mourners," Martin writes, heaping praise on this tender-hearted duo: "Worthy young ladies! You, and such as you, are deserving the regard of the greatest of men. What sisters, what wives, what mothers and what neighbors would you make!—Such a sight as those ladies afforded at that time, and on that occasion, was worthy, and doubtless received the attention of angels."[146] That affecting moment's indelible impression on Martin found its way into his memoir, which was published more than a half-century later and became one of the best-known primary accounts of army life in the Revolution.

FOUR

Perspective

THE SIGNIFICANCE OF THE BATTLE

When Washington dispatched Knowlton's Rangers on their early-morning probe of enemy positions on September 16, 1776—the catalyst for the Battle of Harlem Heights—he was ordering a maneuver that has been likened to poking a stick in a hornet's nest.[1] Then, by launching a counterattack against the British light infantry, he gambled on being able to land a punch without provoking a full retaliatory response, and it is fair to ask whether incurring that risk conflicted with what should have been his first priority—to ensure the preservation of the army that embodied America's quest for independence. The decision to hazard that army by seeking redemption for the embarrassments at Long Island and Kip's Bay derived from Washington's inexperience as a commander, his combative temperament, and what historian John Ferling terms the inner demons that plagued the general.[2]

These considerations are particularly noteworthy given that the Continentals' stand at Harlem Heights did nothing to change the strategic dynamic of the New York campaign and cost the lives of valuable regimental leadership, especially the redoubtable Knowlton and Leitch. That said, this small battle provided a psychological lift—a momentary bright spot in an otherwise dismal New York campaign—to an army that had barely escaped from Brooklyn to Manhattan two weeks previously and had taken flight at Kip's Bay just the day before. Although it probably stemmed in part from the ration of beef issued that night to soldiers who in some cases had not eaten for two days, the boost in morale ensued more from the performance of those who fought against some of the finest in the King's army and the good cheer they shared with the men who had occupied the defensive lines behind them.[3]

Any aura of invincibility that might have attached to His Majesty's forces had been pierced.[4] These citizen-soldiers saw for the first time that they could push back the enemy's best troops and make them turn tail, as Colonel Henry Knox apprised his brother: "The affair of last Monday has had some good consequences toward raising the peoples spirits—they find that if they stick to these mighty men they will run as fast as other people."[5]

As for the commander-in-chief, he took heart from his soldiers' determined resistance on the 16th and the positive, if fleeting, impact on their spirits, writing to John Hancock: "This Affair I am in hopes will be attended with many salutary consequences, as It seems to have greatly inspirited the whole of our Troops."[6] In a letter to his wife the day after the clash, Joseph Reed assured her that "it has given another Face of Things in our Army—the Men have recovered their Spirits & feel a Confidence which before they had quite lost. . . . I do not mean that I think the Enemy have suffered a Loss which will affect their operations—but it has given Spirits to our Men that I hope they will now look the Enemy in the Face with Confidence."[7] His follow-up to her five days later added that the event "hardly deserves the Name of a Battle, but as it was a Scene so different from what had happened the Day before it elevated our Troops very much & in that Respect has been of great Service."[8] Captain John Gooch of Rhode Island, a friend of Nathanael Greene serving with the 9th Continental Regiment, opined one week after the battle that the advantages "the Enemy had, when considered, makes the Victory Glorious, and tho' but over a part of their Army yet the Consequences are attended with Advantages very great, as they immediately quitted the hights all round us and have not been troublesome since. . . . I'm now Ready to give them the second part whenever they have an appetite, as I'm convinced whenever [they] stir from the ships we shall drubb them."[9]

According to Henry P. Johnston, the Continental rank and file would have accorded this encounter a prominent place among the events of 1776 given their own animated descriptions of what occurred and the successful outcome. It would, he believed, have been more than merely an isolated incident in that year's campaign but rather left an indelible impression on an army that was unexpectedly roused from despondency and reassured of its vitality and potential.[10]

Coverage of this affair by most American newspapers during the weeks following reinforced the sense that the rebel cause had been given a new lease on life. The reports provided in such periodicals as the *Independent Chronicle* (September 24), the *Virginia Gazette* (October 4), and the *Newport Mercury* (October 7) omitted mention of the fiasco at Kip's Bay in favor of the victory the following day and eulogized Knowlton as the newest Patriot martyr-hero.[11]

The significance of September 16, 1776, was twofold. First, it marked the earliest battlefield success of the Continental Army. Second, a concerted effort that transcended regional factionalism by units from New England, Maryland, and Virginia—whose men lacked any sense of national identity prior to the Revolution—confirmed that Washington was slowly if painfully creating a national army that could, under the right circumstances, stand up to the Crown's regulars. Here was a foretaste of the resilient fighting force that the commander-in-chief and his generals would gradually mold over the course of a prolonged war of attrition. This day indicated the potential for a fledgling army to effectively coalesce around a common national purpose and affiliation and become the primary instrument for securing American independence. Perhaps it was in this moment that the process of which Washington spoke in his farewell address to the army at war's end seven years later first became apparent: "Who that was not a witness could imagine, that the most violent local prejudices would cease so soon, and that Men who came from different parts of the Continent, strongly disposed by the habits of education, to despise and quarrel with each other, would instantly become but one patriotic band of Brothers?"[12] Instant it was not, but the sentiment is noteworthy just the same.

The fray at Harlem Heights augured the emergence of a military force that would ultimately carry the rebellion on its back—with a necessary back brace in the form of French military and naval assistance. The army's growing capacity over time to cope with hardship and to resist the enemy more effectively helped make the Continentals the center of wartime opposition to British authority. Relative to the rest of American society, they endured a unique degree of service and sacrifice in the Revolutionary enterprise, and those on the home front recognized this as evinced by the interest and anxiety with which they followed the accounts of combat and signified their curiosity as spectators.[13]

In that context, this small battle provided valuable combat experience for some of the rebel combatants that hardened them for the long struggle ahead, as these novice warriors were compelled to acclimate themselves to the reality of an austere military existence. Joseph Plumb Martin illustrated this in his recollection of an incident in his regiment following the engagement: "While standing on the field, after the action had ceased," one of the men complained of being hungry and the officer nearby, "putting his hand into his coat pocket, took out a piece of an ear of Indian corn, burnt as black as a coal, 'Here,' said he to the man complaining, 'eat this and learn to be a soldier.'"[14] One hundred years later, in remarks delivered to the New York Historical Society to mark the centennial of this affair, John Jay II, grandson of the Founding Father John Jay, asserted its importance in developing "the bravery and spirit of our newly levied troops, and their ability, when fairly led, to meet in the open field the flower of the English army and the trained veterans of the Continent."[15]

THE CURTAIN LOWERS ON 1776

In the days following the battle, Washington's troops labored furiously to strengthen their defenses on Harlem Heights. Notwithstanding their transient moment of success, this formidable line of defense along the high ground of upper Manhattan could not assure security on an island surrounded by navigable waters that were dominated by British warships. General Howe continued to eschew a frontal assault against the fortified rebel positions on the heights and did not renew his offensive for several weeks. Presumably impressed by the energetic resistance his forces encountered on September 16 and still bedeviled by the ghosts of Bunker Hill, he instead looked to outflank the defenders by landing troops on the Westchester County coast so as to close off the possibility of any American retreat to the mainland.

Washington had by now been granted tacit authorization by Congress to withdraw from Manhattan, but he did not do so for another month after the Harlem Heights engagement. When he finally did, the Patriot string of setbacks—interrupted only by September 16—continued with the retreat through Westchester County, the abandonment of White Plains after the battle there on October 28, and most impactfully the loss of Fort Washington that was the rebels' last position on Manhattan Island on November 16. General Howe's capture of the fort capped his New York campaign and handed the Americans one of their worst defeats of the entire war, costing them 2,800 soldiers, 140 brass and iron cannon, and a substantial quantity of small arms and ammunition.

On top of the material loss at Fort Washington, deplorable conditions awaited those taken prisoner, two-thirds of whom would perish from disease, exposure, or malnutrition over the next eighteen months. Thomas Knowlton's older brother Daniel, serving as an ensign with the Rangers, and the remnants of his unit were among the captives, effectively ending the service of that contingent. Washington reflected on the significance of this setback in writing to John Hancock: "The Loss of such a Number of Officers and Men, many of whom have been trained with more than common Attention, will I fear be severely felt. But when that of the Arms and Accoutrements is added much more so."[16]

With their New York campaign successfully concluded, the British aimed to forage in New Jersey but also discerned an opportunity to drive Washington's army beyond its boundaries and liberate the state's Loyalist population from rebel rule. During their retreat across the state, the exhausted Continentals presented "a wretched spectacle," according to one of their officers, "without cavalry—but partially provided with artillery—deficient in transport for the little we had to carry—without tents, tools, or camp equipage—without magazines of any kind—half-clothed—badly armed—debilitated by disease, disheartened by misfortune, and worn out with fatigues."[17]

By December 8, Washington's force had crossed to the Pennsylvania side of the Delaware River, now down to about 10 percent of its original strength due to casualties, disease, desertions, and expired enlistments. Moreover, Washington faced the prospect of large-scale departures among his remaining men when their one-year enlistments ran out on December 31. Many were without blankets, winter clothing, shoes, and stockings in the face of freezing temperatures. They were exhausted, hungry, tattered, and painfully aware of having lost every major action to date. The circumstances in which the Continental units found themselves, as reported by British intelligence, may have lulled their adversary into a false sense of security. General James Grant, commanding His Majesty's forces in New Jersey, sought to assure Colonel Johann Rall, in charge of the German brigade occupying Trenton, that an attack by the rebel forces in Pennsylvania was doubtful as they "have neither shoes nor stockings, are in fact almost naked, dying of cold, without blankets and very ill supplied with Provisions."[18]

Desperate to restore the spirits of his soldiery, especially those whose enlistments were to expire at year's end, and of Revolutionary advocates in the general population, Washington and his generals planned an assault on Rall's troops that the commander-in-chief insisted, "necessity, dire necessity will—nay must justify."[19] On Christmas Day 1776, the Continentals crossed an ice-laden Delaware River and marched to Trenton "in a very severe Night, and . . . thro' a violent Storm of Snow and Hail."[20] According to Washington, "The Officers & Men who were engaged in the Enterprize behaved with great firmness, perseverance & bravery and such as did them the highest honour."[21] The ensuing victory over the German garrison was the first major battlefield success enjoyed by Washington's army and the beginning of the "Ten Crucial Days" campaign. What became a legendary winter offensive dramatically altered the course of a military struggle that would not formally end for another seven years, and Lord George Germain conceded as much when he confessed to Parliament, "all our hopes were blasted by that unhappy affair at Trenton."[22]

THE MEASURE OF THOMAS KNOWLTON

In his vignette of Knowlton's life published in 1861, Ashbel Woodward lamented that no effort had been made by the nation or the state of Connecticut "to honor the name of the man who, at the first note of warning, drew the sword for liberty, never laying it aside until his arm was cold in death," and that those "living in the midst of the prosperity purchased at so great cost of revolutionary suffering and revolutionary blood, [had not] reared for him any monument to tell the world that her defenders are embalmed in perpetual remembrance."[23] Almost a decade after Dr. Woodward's death, his call for a monument was finally answered.

In 1893, the Connecticut General Assembly approved a resolution authorizing the State Commission of Sculpture "to have prepared and constructed a suitable memorial . . . to be placed in the Capitol or erected upon the Capitol grounds, to commemorate the gallant service and heroic death, in the war of the Revolution, of Col. Thomas Knowlton of Ashford." The state's lawmakers appropriated $7,500 for this purpose.[24]

The Knowlton memorial was dedicated on November 13, 1895. Sixteen feet four inches in height, the monument stands on the southeast corner of the state capitol grounds in Hartford near the corner of Trinity Street and Capitol Avenue. Its eight-foot-high bronze statue rises above a four-inch-thick plinth that sits atop an eight-foot-high granite pedestal. The facial features of its subject are informed by the image of the man in John Trumbull's painting of the Battle of Bunker Hill, and the appearance it conveys of Knowlton standing defiant with sword in hand is well suited to an officer who was rarely seen without a polished cutlass hanging from his hip.[25]

The following is inscribed on a bronze tablet on the east side of the statue's pedestal: "In memory of Colonel Thomas Knowlton of Ashford Conn. who as a boy served in several campaigns in the French and Indian Wars, shared in the siege and capture of Havana in 1762, was in immediate command of Connecticut troops at the Battle of Bunker Hill, was with his commands closely attached to the person of Washington, and was killed at the Battle of Harlem Heights, September 16, 1776, at the age of thirty-six." (Knowlton was actually two months shy of turning thirty-six when he died.)

The statue was created by Enoch Smith Woods of Hartford, who had sculpted an eight-foot-high bronze figure of Nathan Hale dedicated in 1893, which stands in front of the Wadsworth Atheneum Museum of Art not far from Woods's representation of Knowlton. The bronze was cast by M. H. Mosman of Chicopee, Massachusetts, and the pedestal was designed by Henry Bryant and made by the New England Granite Company. It would appear an instance of fitting artistic symmetry that the same sculptor created memorials to two men inextricably tied to each other in service to the cause of American independence.

At the dedication ceremony for the Knowlton statue in the Hall of the House of Representatives, Governor O. Vincent Coffin endorsed the decision "to place in conspicuous position upon these grounds this statue of the brave and patriotic Knowlton."[26] Patrick Henry Woodward, Ashbel Woodward's son, delivered what was billed as a "historical address" in which he recounted the life of his father's biographical subject in great detail with emphasis on his Revolutionary exploits. "Through this statue," the speaker observed, "the state proclaims that the heroism of her sons shall ever be held in grateful remembrance; that in the sweep of time the dearest rewards are held for noble deeds."[27]

A century after the state of Connecticut gave its blessing to a statue of Knowlton, the professional association of the United States Army's Military Intelligence Corps, which embraces the army's various military intelligence components and their personnel, created an award program in his name. It is part of a legacy reflected in the date 1776 on the Army's Intelligence Seal, which denotes the formation of Knowlton's Rangers as the forerunner of its intelligence branch. In June 1995, the Military Intelligence Corps Association established the "Knowlton Award" in the colonel's honor to recognize association members—including officers and enlisted soldiers (active duty, reserve, or retired) as well as civilians—who have contributed significantly to the promotion of military intelligence in ways that stand out in the eyes of the recipients, their superiors, subordinates, and peers. To qualify, one must have made significant contributions to the corps and demonstrated excellence in military intelligence or support therefor while exhibiting the highest standards of integrity, moral character, and dedication to duty as well as outstanding professional competence and leadership in a military intelligence unit.[28] This is a once-in-a-lifetime award and confers upon a recipient the Knowlton Award Medal featuring a medallion, ribbon, and collar pin.

The Knowlton descendant Judge Samuel Utley once told a story about a young daughter of Thomas Knowlton who, during a horseback ride, met a gentleman who inquired whether she was a daughter of the colonel and commented on her resemblance to the latter. Upon her return home, it is said, she reported the encounter, saying with some indignation "it was that damn Knowlton nose."[29] Fortunately for her father's historical reputation, those who knew him were impressed by more than his proboscis.

Ashbel Woodward's judgment of Knowlton in his biographical sketch, which relies on the collective memories of those who knew the colonel, recalls him as being "courteous and affable in manners, and wholly free from ostentation and egotism," and as a soldier "calm and collected in battle, and, if necessity required, ready to lead where any could be found to follow." He describes the man from Ashford as "the favorite of superior officers, the idol of his soldiers and fellow-townsmen[, who] fell universally lamented." Woodward tells the story of another chance meeting, this one a half-century after Knowlton's death, between a grandson of his traveling in New Hampshire and a Revolutionary War veteran who was relating his combat experience and mentioned that he had fought under the colonel at Harlem Heights. When the old soldier learned that this visitor was a descendant of Knowlton, he insisted that the young man be his guest for the night. He spoke of his former superior officer as "the mildest and most agreeable man he ever knew—that nothing of a rough or harsh nature ever passed his lips—that he was universally respected by those under his command as well as those associated with him."[30]

Thirty-one-years and eight months after the Battle of Harlem Heights, Thomas Knowlton's wife Anna was laid to rest in the family burial plot at Westford Hill Cemetery in Ashford. The inscription on the tombstone reads:

THIS MONUMENT
IS ERECTED IN MEMORY OF
COLONEL THOMAS KNOWLTON AND HIS WIFE.

That brave Colonel, in defense of his Country, fell in battle September 16, 1776, at Harlem Heights, Island of New York, Age 36 years. Mrs Anna, the amiable Consort of Colonel Knowlton, died May 22, 1808, Age 64, and is buried beneath this Monument.

"Remember God did us part,
Accept it with a willing heart."

In addition to Anna, his seven children, and the farm, Knowlton left behind an inventory of possessions amounting to £764. These included: notes against twenty-six individuals; about £101 that he inherited from his parents; clothing valued at £30, including four military suits and some equipment; three military books; a book of music; a book of arithmetic; four small histories; and several Bibles and other volumes.[31] Most of the seven children of Thomas and Anna who made it to adulthood survived well into the nineteenth century: Frederick (1760–1841), Sally (1763–1852), Thomas (1765–1858), Polly (1767–1845), Abigail (1768–1843), Anna (1773–1817), and Lucinda (1776–1805).

The descendants of Captain William Knowlton of England and his three sons who came to America in the 1630s multiplied exponentially over time and left their mark on American life, whether in society, business, the professions, or the military. Perhaps the most notable example is Thomas's grandnephew Nathaniel Lyon, born in Ashford, Connecticut, in 1818 and a West Point graduate and career military officer decorated for his service during the Mexican-American War (1846–1848). He became a Civil War hero as the first Union general killed in the struggle against the Confederacy at the Battle of Wilson's Creek, Missouri, on August 10, 1861. Shortly before the nation's bicentennial, a great-great-great-great-grandson of Thomas Knowlton, Gifford Smith of Waterford, Connecticut, commissioned a painting of the colonel's death at Harlem Heights. Working from accounts of the engagement and Trumbull's depiction of Knowlton at Bunker Hill, artist Lloyd Garrison of New Jersey created an image of the fallen hero as he lay mortally wounded near the scene of battle. His work was featured in the January 1976 issue of the *Connecticut Bicentennial Gazette* published by the American Revolution Bicentennial Commission of Connecticut.[32]

Thomas Knowlton's service to the Revolutionary enterprise over a period of only seventeen months earned him not only a series of promotions—from captain to major to lieutenant colonel—but the respect, admiration, and acclaim of his commander-in-chief and many others with whom he served. His actions arguably merit as much recognition as those of two more celebrated Patriot martyrs—both essentially the same age as Knowlton, in their mid-thirties—who also fell in battle in the early days of the conflict and instantly became the subject of wide-spread mourning among those sympathetic to the Revolution: Dr. Joseph Warren, slain at Bunker Hill, and Major General Richard Montgomery, who assumed a key role in the American invasion of Canada and was killed while leading the attack on Quebec City on the last day of 1775. As with Knowlton, both men were esteemed for their leadership qualities and their deaths were widely mourned.

Consider Knowlton's record in the emergent struggle. He led the first armed contingent from outside Massachusetts into that colony to join the militia there in the wake of the opening shots at Lexington and Concord. He devised a novel rail fence that successfully resisted assault at the Battle of Bunker Hill and orchestrated a stubborn defense of his sector against the British attack, which prevented the Americans from being outflanked and enabled Knowlton's men to provide protective cover for the retreat from the rebel redoubt on Breed's Hill. He spearheaded a daring raid against the enemy at Charlestown that largely achieved its objective while barely firing a shot and without losing a single soldier. He organized an elite intelligence and reconnaissance unit at Washington's direction that has earned Knowlton recognition as the father of American military intelligence, and which included the young Captain Nathan Hale whom posterity crowned with the laurels of legendary heroism. And finally he created the opportunity for, and helped lead, a successful counterattack at Harlem Heights that repelled the British in open-field combat for the first time and boosted the faltering confidence of Washington's army.[33]

Thomas Knowlton's intimate association with the Battle of Harlem Heights suggests just how noteworthy, if largely unrecognized, his role was in the nascent stages of American military history. This uncelebrated event is inextricably intertwined with the leadership he displayed and the resilience of the men he commanded and inspired, arguably more so than with anyone else, as Knowlton's Rangers were the unit in Washington's army who singularly brought on the engagement. The role they and their

Patriot brethren played on September 16, 1776, is especially significant when viewed in a much larger context. These citizen-soldiers carved a distinctive legacy for themselves by the precedent set that day, for no matter how many times U.S. Army troops have recorded a battlefield success over the past two and a half centuries—whether on American soil, in a European wood, across a Middle Eastern desert, or on a Pacific island—one thing about that history remains indisputable. They did it first at Harlem Heights.

Notes

CHAPTER ONE: AN UNEQUAL CONTEST

1. Holger Hoock, *Scars of Independence: America's Violent Birth* (New York: Crown, 2017), 89.

2. Henry P. Johnston, *The Campaign of 1776 Around New York and Brooklyn. Including a New and Circumstantial Account of the Battle of Long Island and the Loss of New York, with a Review of Events to the Close of the Year* (Brooklyn, NY: Long Island Historical Society, 1878), Part 1:104–105.

3. David Hackett Fischer, *Washington's Crossing* (New York: Oxford University Press, 2004), 19–21.

4. General Orders, July 4, 1775, in George Washington, *This Glorious Struggle: George Washington's Revolutionary War Letters.* ed. Edward G. Lengel (Charlottesville: University Press of Virginia, 2007), 9–10.

5. William Howe, *The Narrative of Lieut. Gen. Sir William Howe, in a Committee of the House of Commons, on the 29th of April, 1779, Relative to His Conduct, during His Late Command of the King's Troops in North America: To which are added some Observations upon a Pamphlet, entitled Letters to a Nobleman* (London: H. Baldwin, 1780. Reprint: Toronto Public Library), 3.

6. Rick Atkinson, *The British Are Coming: The War for America, Lexington to Princeton, 1775–1777* (New York: Henry Holt, 2019), 357.

7. David McCullough, *1776* (New York: Simon & Schuster, 2005), 122.

8. Joseph J. Ellis, *Revolutionary Summer: The Birth of American Independence* (New York: Alfred A. Knopf, 2013), 35.

9. Fischer, 31.

10. Ibid., 52.

11. Ibid., 66.

12. Ibid., 33.

13. George Washington to John Hancock, July 10, 1776, in Washington, *This Glorious Struggle*, 52–53.

14. Edward G. Lengel, *General George Washington: A Military Life* (New York: Random House, 2005), 139.

15. Thomas Jefferson to Henry Lee, May 8, 1825, in *The Spirit of 'Seventy-Six: The Story of the American Revolution as Told by Participants*, ed. Henry Steele Commager and Richard B. Morris (New York: Harper & Row, 1967), 315.

16. Ambrose Serle, Journal, July 12–13, 1776, in *The American Revolution: Writings from the War of Independence, 1775–1783*, ed. John Rhodehamel (New York: Library of America, 2001), 142–143.

17. Isaac Bangs, *Journal of Lieutenant Isaac Bangs, April 1 to July 29, 1776*, ed. Edward Bangs (Cambridge, MA: John Wilson and Son, 1890), 57.

18. Fischer, 83. Congress had ordered General Lee south to oversee efforts to strengthen defenses against a possible British assault there, and he proceeded to Baltimore, Norfolk, and then Charleston where he was in command during the failed British attack in the Battle of Sullivan's Island on June 28. Congress ordered Lee to return to New York on August 8, but he did not rejoin Washington's army until after the Battle of Harlem Heights.

19. Nathanael Greene to George Washington, July 11, 1776, in *The Papers of General Nathanael Greene*, ed. Richard K. Showman, vol. 1 (Chapel Hill: University of North Carolina Press, 1976), 252.

20. Theodore Thayer, "Nathanael Greene: Revolutionary War Strategist," in *George Washington's Generals*, ed. George Athan Billias (New York: William Morrow, 1964), 109.

21. McCullough, 153. Sullivan would be captured at the Battle of Long Island but released shortly afterward as part of a prisoner exchange.

22. Ibid., 160.

23. Fischer, 91.

24. Gerald M. Carbone, *Washington: Lessons in Leadership* (New York: Palgrave Macmillan, 2010), 85.

25. George Washington to Lund Washington, August 26, 1776, in Washington, *This Glorious Struggle*, 59.

26. Fischer, 93.

27. Andrew Jackson O'Shaughnessy, *The Men Who Lost America: British Leadership, the American Revolution, and the Fate of the Empire* (New Haven, CT: Yale University Press, 2013), 216.

28. Carbone, 24.

29. O'Shaughnessy, 218.

30. Atkinson, 364.

31. O'Shaughnessy, 92.

32. John J. Gallagher, *The Battle of Brooklyn, 1776* (New York: Da Capo Press, 1995), 129–130.

33. Atkinson, 372.

34. William B. Willcox, "Sir Henry Clinton: Paralysis of Command," in *George Washington's Opponents: British Generals and Admirals in the American Revolutions*, ed. George Athan Billias (New York: William Morrow, 1969), 78.

35. Enoch Anderson, *Personal Recollections of Captain Enoch Anderson* (Wilmington: Historical Society of Delaware, 1896. Reprint: New York Times and Arno Press, 1971), 21–22.

36. Fischer, 98.

37. Henry R. Stiles, *History of the City of Brooklyn, N.Y.* Vol. 1 (Brooklyn, NY: Published by Subscription, 1867), 281–282, n2.

38. Schecter, *The Battle for New York: The City at the Heart of the American Revolution* (New York: Walker & Company, 2002), 153.

39. Maldwyn A. Jones, "Sir William Howe: Conventional Strategist," in *George Washington's Opponents: British Generals and Admirals in the American Revolutions*, 52.

40. George Washington to John Hancock, September 2, 1776, in Washington, *This Glorious Struggle*, 63.

41. Ambrose Serle, Journal, August 27, 1776, in Rhodehamel, 197.

42. Howe, 4–5.

43. Gallagher, 154.

44. Michael Stephenson, *Patriot Battles: How the War of Independence Was Fought* (New York: Harper Perennial, 2008), 242.

45. George Washington to John Hancock, September 2, 1776, in Washington, *This Glorious Struggle*, 63.

46. George Washington to John Hancock, September 8, 1776, in ibid., 64.

47. Ambrose Serle, Journal, September 2, 1776, in Rhodehamel, 204–205.

48. John Haslet to Caesar Rodney, August 31, 1776, in Caesar Rodney, *Letters to and from Caesar Rodney, 1756–1784*, ed. George Herbert Ryden (Philadelphia: Historical Society of Philadelphia, 1933), 108–109.

49. Nathanael Greene to George Washington, September 5, 1776, in Showman, 294–295.

50. George Washington to John Hancock, September 2, 1776, in Washington, *This Glorious Struggle*, 63–64.

51. Bruce Bliven, Jr., *Battle for Manhattan* (New York: Henry Holt and Company, 1956; reprint: Literary Licensing, LLC, 2012), 14.

52. George Washington to John Hancock, September 8, 1776, in Washington, *This Glorious Struggle*, 66.

53. Howe, 5.

54. Ambrose Serle, Journal, September 7, 1776, in Rhodehamel, 210.

55. Frederick MacKenzie, Diary, September 9, 1776, in Commager, 461–462.

56. William R. Shepherd, *The Battle of Harlem Heights* (New York: G. P. Putnam's Sons, 1898), 16.

57. Ambrose Serle, Journal, September 13, 1776, in Rhodehamel, 214.

58. Ambrose Serle, Journal, September 14, 1776, in ibid., 216.

59. General Howe's Orderly Book, September 13, 1776, in Commager, 461.

60. Robert Middlekauff, *The Glorious Cause: The American Revolution, 1763–1789* (New York: Oxford University Press, 2005), 354.

61. Joseph Reed to Mrs. Reed, September 14, 1776, in William B. Reed, *Life and Correspondence of Joseph Reed, Military Secretary of Washington at Cambridge; Adjutant-General of the Continental Army; Member of the Congress of the United States; and President of the Executive Council of the State of Pennsylvania*, vol. 1 (Philadelphia: Lindsay and Blakiston, 1847; reprint: Adamant Media Corporation, 2006), 235. Reed, then Washington's closest confidant, was a thirty-three-year-old Philadelphia lawyer who had served as the general's first military secretary during the

siege of Boston and then taken a leave of absence to attend to personal matters before being lured back into service by Washington's offer to become the army's lead administrator with a generous salary.

62. Ambrose Serle, Journal, September 13, 1776, in Rhodehamel, 215.

63. Ibid., 217.

64. Ibid.

65. Bliven, 27, and Atkinson, 389.

66. Ambrose Serle Journal, September 15, 1776, in Rhodehamel, 217.

67. Joseph Plumb Martin, *Memoir of a Revolutionary Soldier: The Narrative of Joseph Plumb Martin* (Mineola, NY: Dover Publications, 2006), 20.

68. Benjamin Trumbull, Journal, September 15, 1776, in Rhodehamel, 222. Grapeshot and canister were exploding shells of different sizes—in the form of a tin can and canvas bag, respectively—packed with objects such as iron balls, nails, pieces of chain, or stones.

69. Frederick Mackenzie, Diary, September 9, 1776, in Commager, 462.

70. Caroline Cox, *A Proper Sense of Honor: Service and Sacrifice in George Washington's Army* (Chapel Hill: University of North Carolina Press, 2004), 55.

71. William Howe to George Germain, September 21, 1776, in Henry P. Johnston, *The Battle of Harlem Heights, September 16, 1776; With a Review of the Events of the Campaign* (New York: Macmillan Company, 1897; reprint: Franklin Classics, 2018), 202–203.

72. Atkinson, 390.

73. Regarding grenadiers, see Hagist, *These Distinguished Corps*, 11. Christopher L. Ward, *The Delaware Continentals, 1776–1783* (Wilmington: Historical Society of Delaware, 1941), 51–52.

74. John Ferling, *Almost a Miracle: The American Victory in the War of Independence* (New York: Oxford University Press, 2007), 141.

75. Bliven, 18 and 26, and Schecter, 181.

76. George Washington to John Hancock, September 16, 1776, in Washington, *This Glorious Struggle*, 67–68.

77. James Thacher, *A Military Journal During the American Revolutionary War, from 1775 to 1783, Describing Interesting Events and Transactions of This Period, with Numerous Historical Facts and Anecdotes, from the Original Manuscript* (Boston: Richardson and Lord, 1823), 69–70.

78. Nathaniel Philbrick, *Valiant Ambition: George Washington, Benedict Arnold, and the Fate of the American Revolution* (New York: Viking, 2016), 68.

79. Schecter, 181, and Bliven, 30.

80. Martin, 20–21.

81. Bliven, 37.

82. Bliven, 34–35; Schecter, 183–184.

83. William Heath, *Memoirs of Major-General William Heath*, ed. William Abbatt (New York: William Abbatt, 1901; reprint: Sagwan Press, 2015), 52.

84. Atkinson, 393.

85. Bliven, 20–21.

86. Ibid., 38–39.

87. Schecter, 189.

88. William Tryon was Royal Governor of New York from 1771 to 1780, after serving as Royal Governor of North Carolina from 1765 to 1771. Thacher, 70–71.

89. Stephenson, 246.

90. Bliven, 60–61.

91. Schecter, 189–190.

92. Johnston, *The Battle of Harlem Heights*, 40.

93. Bliven, 58.

94. Ferling, 141.

95. Bliven, 57–58.

96. Ibid., 52. Burr came from a prominent New Jersey family and graduated from the College of New Jersey (Princeton University today) at age sixteen. Interrupting his legal studies to join the Continental Army, he rose to the rank of lieutenant colonel before resigning from the army in 1779 due to ill health. Burr later served as a member of the New York State Assembly, state attorney general, U.S. Senator, and third vice president of the United States (1801–1805), but is probably best known for fatally wounding his political rival Alexander Hamilton in a duel in 1804.

97. Ibid., 63.

98. Patrick K. O'Donnell, *Washington's Immortals: The Untold Story of an Elite Regiment Who Changed the Course of the Revolution* (New York: Atlantic Monthly Press, 2016), 80.

99. Ibid., 15–16. Continental Army regiments were often referred to by the name of a regimental colonel rather than their numerical designation, even when that officer had been captured or promoted.

100. William Smallwood to Tench Tilghman, October 12, 1776, in *Journal and Correspondence of the Maryland Council of Safety, July 7: December 31, 1776*, Archives of Maryland Online, 12:342. https://msa.maryland.gov/megafile/msa/speccol/sc2900/sc2908/000001/000012/html/am12—342.html.

101. Fischer, 197.

102. Account of the Retreat from New York and Affair of Harlem Heights, by Colonel David Humphreys, in Johnston, *The Campaign of 1776 Around New York and Brooklyn*, Part 2:90.

103. Bliven, 53.

104. George Washington to John Hancock, September 16, 1776, in Washington, *This Glorious Struggle*, 68.

105. Benjamin Trumbull, Journal, September 15, 1776, in Rhodehamel, 223.

106. Ambrose Serle Journal, September 15, 1776, in ibid., 217–218.

107. Alan Taylor, *American Revolutions: A Continental History, 1750–1804* (New York: W. W. Norton, 2016), 165. See also Atkinson, 394.

108. Ellis, 152.

109. Philip Vickers Fithian, Journal, September 15, 1776, in Rhodehamel, 220–221.

110. Ron Chernow, *Washington: A Life* (New York: Penguin Press, 2010), 254.

CHAPTER TWO: THE RISE OF THOMAS KNOWLTON

1. Johnston, *The Battle of Harlem Heights*, 52.

2. Terry Crowdy, *The Enemy Within: A History of Espionage* (New York: Osprey Publishing, 2006), 94.

3. Middlekauff, 356.

4. M. William Phelps, *Nathan Hale: The Life and Death of America's First Spy* (New York: Thomas Dunne Books, 2008), 134.

5. Schecter, 197.

6. Rev. Charles Henry Wright Stocking, D.D., *The History and Genealogy of the Knowltons of England and America*, vol. 1 (New York: Knickerbocker Press, 1897; reprint: Wentworth Press, 2016), 92.

7. George Washington's Address to Congress, June 16, 1775, in *This Glorious Struggle*, 4.

8. Author's Note, in W. F. Morgan, Jr., "Army Intelligence Heritage Series: LTC Thomas Knowlton Biography and Sources Revisited," *The Vanguard: Journal of the Military Intelligence Corps Association* 15, no. 2 (April 2010), 21.

9. Historical Address by P. Henry Woodward, in Patrick Henry Woodward, *Statute of Colonel Thomas Knowlton: Ceremonies at the Unveiling* (Hartford, CT: Press of the Case, Lockwood & Brainard Company, 1895. Reprint: Franklin Classics, 2018), 9n. Ashbel Woodward was born and raised in Ashford and befriended Minor Knowlton and his brother Danford, grandnephews of Thomas Knowlton, and William W. Marcy, who married a granddaughter of Thomas Knowlton. Woodward's friends assisted him in collecting information about Thomas Knowlton and those who knew him and eventually turned those papers over to Woodward.

10. Ashbel Woodward, *Memoir of Col. Thomas Knowlton, of Ashford, Connecticut* (Boston: Henry W. Dutton & Son, 1861; reprint: Andesite Press, 2015), 3.

11. David Thorp, Military Pension Application Narrative, in Johnston, *The Battle of Harlem Heights*, 195.

12. Walter R. Borneman, *American Spring: Lexington, Concord, and the Road to Revolution* (New York: Little, Brown, 2014), 350. Borneman contends that "since the name Breed's Hill was apparently not known in 1775, it seems correct to say that the Battle of Bunker Hill was indeed fought on the broader slopes of what everyone at the time thought was Bunker Hill. The crest at the center of the action only became known as Breed's Hill shortly thereafter." For confirmation that the pastures at the scene of the battle were not yet named Breed's Hill, see also Richard Frothingham, Jr., *History of the Siege of Boston, and of the Battles of Lexington, Concord, and Bunker Hill* (Boston: Little, Brown, 1873), 119. Noting that "Breed's Hill" is not named in any description of streets before 1775, Frothingham adds: "This tract of land was called after the owners of the pastures into which it was divided, rather than by the common name of Breed's Hill." Notwithstanding these observations, there appears to be a consensus among historians that the fighting occurred at Breed's Hill and therefore the commonplace reference to the "Battle of Bunker Hill" is a misnomer.

13. John Trumbull, *Autobiography, Reminiscences and Letters of John Trumbull, from 1756 to 1841* (New York: Wiley and Putnam, 1841), 20–21.

14. Paul Staiti, *Of Arms and Artists: The American Revolution through Painters' Eyes* (New York: Bloomsbury Press, 2016), 177. For John Trumbull passion for the cause of American independence was a family affair. His father Jonathan was

the only colonial governor to support the rebellion against Great Britain and a friend and advisor to George Washington. One of John's brothers, Joseph, served as the Continental Army's commissary general in the early phase of the war; and another brother, Jonathan Jr., was the army's paymaster and later a military secretary to Washington. John lent more than his artistic talents to promoting the enterprise, serving first as an aide-de-camp to Washington and then as a brigade major in the army during the siege of Boston in 1775–1776 before following the American troops to New York. He eventually became a colonel but resigned from the army in early 1777 over a misunderstanding with Congress about the starting date of his commission in that rank.

15. Abigail Adams to Elizabeth Smith Shaw, March 4, 1786. *Founders Online*, National Archives. https://founders.archives.gov/?q=Volume%3AAdams-04-07&s=1511311112&r=22.

16. Arthur Lefkowitz, *Eyewitness Images from the American Revolution* (Gretna, LA: Pelican, 2017), 78.

17. Staiti, 182.

18. John Chester and Samuel B. Webb to Joseph Webb, June 19, 1775, in Rhodehamel, 38. See also Staiti, 182. Warren's body was interred on the battlefield with an anonymous soldier but exhumed in 1777 and reinterred at King's Chapel before a crowd of his fellow Bostonians.

19. Staiti, 184.

20. Hon. Samuel Utley, in Knowlton Association of America, Miner Rockwell Knowlton, and William Herrick Griffith, *Prospectus and Year Book Containing the History, Constitutions, By-laws, List of Officers And Members of the Knowlton Association of America From Its Organization, with an Account of the First and Second Reunions* (Albany, NY: S. H. Wentworth, printer, 1897), 45. Judge Utley's remarks were delivered at the second reunion of the Knowlton Association at the Hotel Vendome in Boston on June 17, 1896 (the anniversary of the Battle of Bunker Hill) and included in the association's first yearbook. The first reunion was held immediately following the unveiling of the statue of Thomas Knowlton on the grounds of the State Capitol in Hartford, Connecticut, on November 13, 1895.

21. Historical Address by P. Henry Woodward, in Patrick Henry Woodward, 37–38.

22. Presentation by Charles Dudley Warner, in ibid., 6.

23. Ellis, 153.

24. Stocking, 49.

25. Ashbel Woodward, 3. This account infers Knowlton's birthdate from church baptismal records, according to which he received the sacrament on November 30, 1740. At that time, the ceremony was customarily performed on the eighth day after birth.

26. Mark Allen Baker, *Spies of Revolutionary Connecticut: From Benedict Arnold to Nathan Hale* (Charleston, SC: History Press, 2014), 78.

27. Bruce C. Daniels, "Economic Development in Colonial and Revolutionary Connecticut: An Overview," *William and Mary Quarterly* 37, no. 3 (July 1980), 432–433.

28. Richard M. Bayles, *History of Windham County, Connecticut* (New York: W. W. Preston & Company, 1889), 998.

29. Col. David Humphreys, *An Essay on the Life of the Honourable Major General Israel Putnam. Addressed to the State Society of the Cincinnati in the State of Connecticut, And first published by their order* (Boston: Samuel Avery, 1818), 20.

30. Lawrence A. Cremin, *American Education: The Colonial Experience, 1607–1783* (New York: Harper & Row, 1970), 500.

31. Ashbel Woodward, 15.

32. Ibid., 15.

33. Phelps, 134.

34. Alexander Rose, *Washington's Spies: The Story of America's First Spy Ring* (New York: Bantam Books, 2014), 16.

35. Fred Anderson, *Crucible of War: The Seven Years' War and the Fate of Empire in British North America, 1754–1766* (New York: Vintage Books, 2000), 136.

36. I. W. Stuart, *Life of Jonathan Trumbull, Sen., Governor of Connecticut* (Boston: Crocker and Brewster, 1859. Reprint: Kessinger Publishing, 2010), 48–49.

37. Fred Anderson, 782n6.

38. Ibid., 768–769n4.

39. John R. Cuneo, *Robert Rogers of the Rangers* (New York: Richardson & Steirman, 1987), 55.

40. Robert Rogers, *Journals of Major Robert Rogers: Containing an Account of the Several Excursions He Made under the Generals Who Commanded upon the Continent of North America during the Late War; from Which May be Collected the Most Material Circumstances of Every Campaign upon That Continent, from the Commencement to the Conclusion of the War; with an Introduction and Notes, and an Appendix Containing Numerous Documents and Papers relating to the Doings of Major Rogers While Commanding at Michilimackinack, in 1767; and His Conduct in the Early Part of the Revolutionary War. By Franklin B. Hough* (Albany, NY: Joel Munsell's Sons, 1883), 82–86.

41. Ibid., 122.

42. Cuneo, 27. By mid-eighteenth century, the colonists had long since adopted with alacrity the Indian practice of scalping enemy dead, encouraged by a well-established tradition of paying bounties for Indian scalps. See Stephenson, 195. See also Peter Oliver, "A Tory View of Frontier Warfare: Summer 1778" from "The Origin & Progress of the American Rebellion," in Rhodehamel, 487–489. Oliver wrote in part: "This Scalping Business hath been encouraged, in the Colonies, for more than a Century past. Premiums have been given, frequently, by the *Massachusetts* Assemblies, for the Scalps of Indians, even when they boasted loudest of their Sanctity; & I have seen a Vessell enter the Harbor of *Boston*, with a long String of hairy Indian Scalps strung to the rigging, & waving in the wind."

43. Ashbel Woodward, 4–5. According to Woodward, the account of Knowlton's exploits at Wood Creek was narrated by his son. He does not specify which one, but presumably it was his oldest, Frederick.

44. Hon. Samuel Utley, in Knowlton Association of America, 48.

45. Ibid., 804n8.

46. Ashbel Woodward, 5.

47. Judge Samuel Utley reported that his great-grandfather Thomas Knowlton

spelled his name "Knolton" in his account book, which was donated to the Connecticut Historical Society (CHS) by William R. Marcy, husband of a granddaughter of Knowlton. See Hon. Samuel Utley, in Knowlton Association of America, 46. The account book is part of the CHS collection today, and the author has viewed several of its pages electronically. The name is spelled "Knolton" in a majority of the entries, but it appears that many of these were written by parties other than Thomas—presumably individuals who received something from him and wrote a receipt in the book. Conversely, in the front and back where there are lists of members of his regiment, the name is written with a "w," but it is uncertain who wrote the lists. This information is based on an email to the author from Elena Peters, Collections Associate at the Connecticut Historical Society, on February 10, 2022. The spelling of the name, as it applied to how Thomas and his brother Daniel were listed on regimental rolls during the French and Indian War, took various forms, including "Knowlton," "Knolton," "Knoulten," and "Nolton." However the family spelled the name at the time, it was obviously subject to creative modifications. The fact that George Washington's Revolutionary War correspondence variously referred to Thomas as "Knolton" or "Knowlton" may say more about the general's penchant for inventive spelling than how Thomas actually wrote his name.

48. "Rare Signature of America's First Head of Military Intelligence." *Between the Covers Rare Books Catalog 211: Americana Part II* [BTC#413461] (Between the Covers Rare Books, 2017), 26–27. https://www.betweenthecovers.com/images/upload/c211.pdf.

49. James Hillhouse to Nathan Hale, July 11, 1774, in *Documentary Life of Nathan Hale, Comprising All Available Official and Private Documents Bearing on the Life of The Patriot, Together with an Appendix, showing the background of his life; including his family circle; his college friends; his friends made as a school-master and in the army; with many illustrations, portraits and buildings that knew his footsteps,* ed. George Dudley Seymour (New Haven, CT: Privately printed, 1941), 21–22.

50. Robert Ernest Hubbard, *Major General Israel Putnam: Hero of the American Revolution* (Jefferson, NC: McFarland, 2017), 64.

51. Bayles, 67. Opinion was deeply divided among Americans in regard to British colonial policy. Across the colonies generally, the Patriot faction was the most vocal and best-organized segment among the general public; however, it accounted for no more than 45 percent of the white male population, while Loyalists comprised perhaps 15 to 20 percent and the rest claimed to be neutral. See Derek W. Beck, *Igniting the American Revolution, 1773–1775* (Naperville, IL: Sourcebooks, 2015), 77.

52. Hon. Samuel Utley, in Knowlton Association of America, 47. See also Ashbel Woodward, 6.

53. Carol Berkin, *Revolutionary Mothers: Women and the Struggle for America's Independence* (New York: Alfred A. Knopf, 2005), 30–33.

54. Stuart, 697.

55. Jonathan Trumbull to Thomas Gage, April 28, 1775, in Stuart, 175.

56. Hubbard, 82.

57. William Prescott to John Adams, August 25, 1775, in Frothingham, 395.

58. Thomas Gage to the Earl of Dartmouth, June 25, 1775, in ibid., 386.

59. John Chester to Joseph Fish, July 22, 1775, in ibid., 390.

60. Bayles, 72.

61. Humphreys, 96–97.

62. Frothingham, 189–190.

63. Jonathan Brigham, Military Pension Application Narrative, in *The Revolution Remembered: Eyewitness Accounts of the War for Independence*, ed. John C. Dann (Chicago: University of Chicago Press, 1980), 4.

64. Letter of a British officer, July 5, 1775, in Commager, 135.

65. Thomas Gage to Lord Barrington, June 26, 1775, in ibid., 134. Friendly fire accounted for an imprecise number of British casualties, as a number of those in the advancing grenadier battalion were killed or wounded by fire from light infantry positioned behind them. Hagist, *These Distinguished Corps*, 33–35.

66. George Washington to Joseph Reed, January 14, 1776. *Founders Online*, National Archives. https://founders.archives.gov?q=Thomas%20Knowlton&s=1511311111&r=8.

67. George Washington to John Hancock, January 11, 1776. *Founders Online*, National Archives. https://founders.archives.gov?q=Thomas%20Knowlton&s=1511311111&r=7.

68. John Adams to Mercy Otis Warren, January 8, 1776. *Founders Online*, National Archives. https://founders.archives.gov?q=Thomas%20Knowlton&s=1511311111&r=1.

69. George Washington to John Hancock, January 11, 1776. *Founders Online*, National Archives. https://founders.archives.gov?q=Thomas%20Knowlton&s=1511311111&r=7.

70. General Orders, January 9, 1776. *Founders Online*, National Archives. https://founders.archives.gov?q=Thomas%20Knowlton&s=1511311111&r=6.

71. McCullough, 74–75.

72. From *The Journal of Gen. Sir Martin Hunter, G.C.M.G., G.C.H., and some Letters of his Wife, Lady Hunter*, in Commager, 166.

73. George Washington to Robert Hunter Morris, January 1, 1756. *Founders Online*, National Archives. https://founders.archives.gov/documents/Washington/02-02-02-0255.

74. Ashbel Woodward, 11.

75. The units that supplied men for Knowlton's Rangers included: three Connecticut Continental regiments—Colonel John Durkee's 20th, Colonel Charles Webb's 19th, and Colonel Samuel Wyllys's 22nd; Colonel Paul Dudley Sargent's 16th Massachusetts Continentals; Colonel Daniel Hitchcock's Rhode Island Continentals; and Colonel John Chester's 6th Connecticut State Levies. Ranger officers were drawn from the following units: Sargent's 16th Massachusetts—Major Andrew Colburn, Captain Lemuel Holmes, First Lieutenant Ephraim Cleveland, First Lieutenant William Scott, First Lieutenant Aaron Stratten, Second Lieutenant Jacob Pope, and Ensign Aaron Cleveland; Webb's 19th Connecticut—Adjutant Thomas Fosdick, Captain Nathan Hale, First Lieutenant Jesse Grant, and Ensign Benoni Shipman; Durkee's 20th Connecticut—Captains Stephen Brown and Thomas Grosvenor and First Lieutenant Oliver Babcock;

Wyllys's 22nd Connecticut—Ensign Thomas Hender; Chester's 6th Connecticut State Levies—First Lieutenant Abner Bacon and Ensign Daniel Knowlton. For a list of the soldiers comprising Knowlton's Rangers, see Johnston, *The Battle of Harlem Heights*, 189–190; Henry P. Johnston, ed., *Record of Connecticut Men in the Military and Naval Service during the War of the Revolution, 1775–1783*. Adjutant-General's Office (Hartford, CT: Case, Lockwood & Brainard Co., 1889); Morgan, 22–23; and "American Wars." *Knowlton's Rangers, 1776*, https://www. americanwars.org/ct-american-revolution/knowltons-rangers-1776.htm.

76. Ashbel Woodward, 13.

77. Bliven, 84.

78. Henry P. Johnston, *The Campaign of 1776 Around New York and Brooklyn*, Part 2:154.

79. Johnston, *The Battle of Harlem Heights*, 54.

80. George Washington to William Heath, September 5, 1776, in George Washington, *The Writings of George Washington from the Original Manuscript Sources*. Vol. 6. Electronic Text Center, University of Virginia Library. https://web.archive. org/web/20110218172145/http://etext.lib.virginia.edu/etcbin/toccer-new2?id=WasFi06.xml&images=images/modeng&data=/texts/english/modeng/parsed&tag=public&part=16&division=div1#n0052-20.

81. Nathan Miller, *Spying for America: The Hidden History of U.S. Intelligence* (New York: Dell Publishing, 1989), 18–19.

82. Jasper Gilbert to Cyrus P. Bradley, January 9, 1836, in Seymour, 339.

83. "General Hull's Account of the Last Hours and Last Words of Hale," in ibid., 308–309.

84. William W. Saltonstall to Cyrus P. Bradley, March 1, 1837, in ibid., 349.

85. Frederick MacKenzie, Diary, September 22, 1776, in Rhodehamel, 229.

86. "General Hull's Account of the Last Hours and Last Words of Hale," in Seymour, 310. Nathan Hale's friend Captain William Hull alleged that John Montresor, a British captain who was present at his execution, informed Alexander Hamilton, then a captain of artillery, when Montresor entered the American camp under a flag of truce, that Hale had been arrested, condemned, and executed—and reported his fabled dying words that quoted from Joseph Addison's 1712 play, a dramatization of the last days of the Roman Senator Marcus Porcius Cato, which was widely read by educated Americans at the time. The Hull manuscripts were compiled by his daughter, Mrs. Maria Campbell, and published in the *Revolutionary Services and Civil Life of William Hull* in 1848. For more than a century afterward, most accounts of Hale's final words conformed to the legend propagated by Hull, such as in John Bakeless, *Turncoats, Traitors and Heroes: Espionage in the American Revolution* (New York: Da Capo Press, 1998), 120–121. In contrast, Rick Atkinson opines that Captain MacKenzie's contemporary account is probably more accurate. See Atkinson, 401. MacKenzie reported Hale's death as he heard it from persons who were present when he was hanged, one of them being Tunis Bogart, a Long Island farmer who was at the artillery park as a wagon driver for the British. See Phelps, 193.

87. Excerpts from the Diary of Enoch Hale, January 25, 1777, in Seymour, 298.

CHAPTER THREE: RECONNAISSANCE AND RESISTANCE

1. Stephenson, 245.

2. Nathanael Greene to Nicholas Cooke, September 17, 1776, in Showman, 300.

3. Nathanael Greene to John Adams, June 2, 1776, in ibid., 224.

4. Benjamin Trumbull, Journal, September 15, 1776, in Rhodehamel, 223.

5. Martin, 24.

6. Henry Knox to William Knox, September 23, 1776, in Francis S. Drake, *Life and Correspondence of Henry Knox, Major-General in the American Revolutionary Army* (Boston: Samuel G. Drake, 1873), 31–32.

7. Account of the Retreat from New York and Affair of Harlem Heights, by Colonel David Humphreys, in Johnston, *The Campaign of 1776 Around New York and Brooklyn,* Part 2:90.

8. Bliven, 67.

9. Samuel Richards, *Diary of Captain Samuel Richards: Connecticut Line, Revolutionary War 1775–1781* (Published by his great-grandson, 1909; reprint: Big Byte Books, 2014), 26.

10. Johnston, *The Battle of Harlem Heights,* 48–49.

11. Philip Vickers Fithian, Journal, September 15, 1776, in Rhodehamel, 221.

12. Ibid., 219.

13. Bliven, 82. Washington's troops generally referred to their encampment as camp "Harlem Heights," although that name was applied well after the war to all the high ground around the Harlem flatlands, including what is now Morningside Heights and the northern end of Central Park. Johnston, *The Battle of Harlem Heights,* 48.

14. Showman, 301–302n2. The reference is to John Nixon of Massachusetts, a veteran of the French and Indian War who saw action with the minute men of Sudbury at Concord on April 19, 1775, became colonel of a Massachusetts regiment, was wounded at Bunker Hill, and commissioned a Continental brigadier general on August 9, 1776. He is not to be confused with the Philadelphia shipping merchant John Nixon, who as a colonel of the Philadelphia Associators militia unit saw action with the Continental Army at the Battle of Princeton in 1777 and was with the army in the Valley Forge winter encampment of 1777–1778.

Beall's men were militia sent by Maryland to serve as part of the "Flying Camp," which had been established by Congress to function as a highly mobile reserve that could be quickly dispatched to any location where needed. These militia were to serve until December 1, 1776, unless discharged sooner by Congress. They joined up with Washington's army shortly after the arrival of the Marylanders in Smallwood's Regiment, into which many of those in the Flying Camp from that state would eventually be merged. Congress designated General Beall as commander of the Maryland militia in the Flying Camp but failed to name an overall commander of the Maryland forces, and Beall and Colonel Smallwood argued about who held the higher rank. O'Donnell, *Washington's Immortals,* 50–52.

15. George Washington to Martha Washington, June 18, 1775, in Washington, *This Glorious Struggle,* 5.

16. Bliven, 81.

17. George Washington to John Hancock, September 16, 1776, in Washington, *This Glorious Struggle*, 68.

18. Schecter, 196.

19. Johnston, *The Battle of Harlem Heights*, 57–58.

20. Bliven, 84–85.

21. Johnston, *The Battle of Harlem Heights*, 59. See also Bliven, 86.

22. Johnston, *The Battle of Harlem Heights*, 45–47.

23. William Howe to George Germain, September 21, 1776, in ibid., 203–204.

24. Ibid., 44–45.

25. Don N. Hagist, *These Distinguished Corps: British Grenadier and Light Infantry Battalions in the American Revolution* (Warwick, UK: Helion & Company, 2021), 64.

26. George Harris to his uncle (date unspecified), in Johnston, *The Battle of Harlem Heights*, 207.

27. The terms "battalion" and "regiment" were virtually synonymous at the time of the Revolution. In both the British and Continental armies, most regiments had only a single battalion. Wright, *The Continental Army*, 435. The 42nd (Royal Highland) Regiment was distinctive in His Majesty's army for its reliance on highland Scots and the fact that it advertised for recruits in the Gaelic language. This unit was exceptional in the sense that British regiments did not otherwise focus their recruiting efforts entirely on particular geographic areas. See Don N. Hagist, *Noble Volunteers: The British Soldiers Who Fought the American Revolution* (Yardley, PA: Westholme, 2020), 26 and 28.

28. Bliven, 89.

29. Recollections of Oliver Burnham, in Johnston, *The Battle of Harlem Heights*, 178. A resident of Cornwall, Connecticut, Burnham was a Ranger drawn from Wyllys's Connecticut Continental Regiment and in later life became a state legislator and judge.

30. Bliven, 87.

31. Judith L. Van Buskirk, *Standing in Their Own Light: African American Patriots in the American Revolution* (Norman: University of Oklahoma Press, 2017), 72–73.

32. Schecter, 145.

33. Bliven, 88–90.

34. Johnston, *The Battle of Harlem Heights*, 61.

35. A Continental officer (probably Stephen Brown) to a friend, September 21, 1776, in ibid., 154–155.

36. Joseph Reed to Mrs. Reed, September 17, 1776, in ibid., 134–135.

37. Ibid., 61.

38. Gold Silliman to Mrs. Silliman, September 17, 1776, in ibid., 149–150. Silliman, a Yale College graduate and an attorney, was colonel of the 1st Connecticut State Levies and later became a brigadier general in the militia.

39. Bliven, 91.

40. George Washington to John Hancock, September 18, 1776. *Founders Online*, National Archives. https://founders.archives.gov/documents/Washington/03-06-02-0264.

41. "George Washington's Mount Vernon." *Battle of Harlem Heights.* Fred W. Smith National Library for the Study of George Washington at Mount Vernon. https://www.mountvernon.org/library/digitalhistory/digital-encyclopedia/article/battle-of-harlem-heights/.

42. Matthew Spring, *With Zeal and with Bayonets Only: The British Army on Campaign in North America, 1775–1783* (Norman: University of Oklahoma Press, 2008), 158–159.

43. Joseph Reed to Mrs. Reed, September 17, 1776, in Johnston, *The Battle of Harlem Heights,* 135.

44. Gallagher, 162–163.

45. George Washington to Patrick Henry, October 5, 1776. *Founders Online,* National Archives. https://founders.archives.gov/?q=George%20Washington%20to%20Patrick%20Henry%20%22to%20recover%20that%20military%20ardour%22&s=1511311111&r=1.

46. Johnston, *The Battle of Harlem Heights,* 75. See also Bliven, 96. Archibald Crary, then twenty-seven, served as colonel of the 2nd Rhode Island Regiment and agent for the War Department in Rhode Island. He was adjutant general of the Rhode Island militia from 1780 to the end of the war and in 1784 won election to the Rhode Island General Assembly.

Andrew Leitch was a twenty-eight-year-old Scottish-born merchant and a resident of Dumfries, Virginia, who had moved from Maryland in 1774. He hosted Washington at his home in March 1775 while a member of the Prince William County committee of correspondence and visited Mount Vernon a month later (Founders Online, National Archives. https://founders.archives.gov/documents/Washington/05-07-02-0156, note). Leitch left his wife and children to join the army, first commissioned as a captain in the 3rd Virginia Regiment in February 1776 and then as a major in the 1st Virginia. He marched to New York with the 3rd Virginia, as they were a few weeks ahead of the 1st Virginia, but did not join up with Washington's army until early September.

The 3rd Virginia Regiment was authorized on December 28, 1775, as a unit of the Continental Army and organized on February 28, 1776, at Alexandria and Dumfries to consist of ten companies from Culpeper, Fairfax, Fauquier, King George, Loudon, Louisa, Prince William, and Stafford Counties. Originally assigned to the Southern Department, the regiment was relieved from the latter and assigned to the main army on July 20, 1776. Wright, *The Continental Army,* 285.

47. John Chilton to "My Friends," September 17, 1776 (Keith Papers, Virginia Historical Society), in George F. Scheer and Hugh F. Rankin, *Rebels and Redcoats: The American Revolution Through the Eyes of Those Who Fought and Lived It* (New York: Da Capo Press, 1987), 185. Chilton was a thirty-seven-year-old tobacco planter from Fauquier County in Virginia who wrote a series of letters about his service in the army. He was mortally wounded at the Battle of Brandywine in 1777.

48. Joseph Reed to Mrs. Reed, September 21, 1776, in Johnston, *The Battle of Harlem Heights,* 135.

49. George Clinton to Peter Tappen, September 21, 1776, in ibid., 143. The fence is presumed to have been at the northern edge of the Hoaglandt farm along today's Broadway between 123rd and 124th Streets. Johnston, *The Battle of Harlem Heights*, 76.

50. Johnston, *The Battle of Harlem Heights*, 76–77. See also Schecter, 199.

51. Joseph Reed to Mrs. Reed, September 22, 1776, in Johnston, *The Battle of Harlem Heights*, 137.

52. Bliven, 95.

53. David Griffiths to Leven Powel, September 18, 1776, in Johnston, *The Battle of Harlem Heights*, 171–172.

54. Excerpt from a letter from an officer to his friend in New London, Connecticut, September 21, 1776, in ibid., 155. Tradition has it that Sergeant Nehemiah Holt was by Knowlton's side when he was shot. Johnston, *The Battle of Harlem Heights*, 192. He was nineteen years of age and like Knowlton a resident of Windham County, Connecticut.

55. David Thorp, Military Pension Application Narrative, in ibid., 195.

56. Joseph Reed to Mrs. Reed, September 17, 1776, in ibid., 135.

57. Margaret MacMillan, *War: How Conflict Shaped Us* (New York: Random House, 2020), 158.

58. Hubbard, 127.

59. Theodore P. Savas and J. David Dameron, *A Guide to the Battles of the American Revolution* (El Dorado Hills, CA: Savas Beatie, 2013), 66.

60. The long list of killed and wounded high-ranking officers on both sides in the Revolution attests to this harsh reality, including, but not limited to: among the British, Generals James Agnew, Charles Cornwallis, Simon Fraser, and Charles O'Hara, and Colonels John Bird and Henry Monckton; and on the American side, Generals Benedict Arnold, Johann deKalb, Hugh Mercer, Richard Montgomery, Francis Nash, Casimir Pulaski, and Nathaniel Woodhull. The 226 British killed at Bunker Hill in 1775 included nineteen officers, and nearly a quarter of the British dead (twenty out of eighty-five) at Eutaw Springs in 1781 were officers. See Stephenson, 71.

61. Richard M. Ketchum, *Decisive Day: The Battle for Bunker Hill* (Garden City, NY: Doubleday & Company, 1974), 153.

62. Charles Royster, *A Revolutionary People at War: The Continental Army and American Character, 1775–1783*, published for the Institute of Early American History and Culture, Williamsburg, VA (Chapel Hill: University of North Carolina Press, 1979), 207–208.

63. George Washington to Patrick Henry, October 5, 1776. *Founders Online*, National Archives. https://founders.archives.gov/?q=George%20Washington%20to%20Patrick%20Henry%20%22to%20recover%20that%20military%20ardour%22&s=1511311111&r=1.

64. Bliven, 96.

65. Johnston, *The Battle of Harlem Heights*, 85.

66. George Washington to John Hancock, September 18, 1776. *Founders Online*, National Archives. https://founders.archives.gov/documents/Washington/03-06-02-0264. These Maryland regiments were composed of militia troops of the "Maryland Flying Camp" authorized by Congress.

67. Ellis, 184. See also Richard M. Ketchum, *The Winter Soldiers* (Garden City, NY: Doubleday & Company, Inc., 1973), 224–225. An extensive analysis of the factors that influenced the outcome of the war is provided in chapter 25 in Ferling, 562–575, and the conclusion in O'Shaughnessy, 353–361.

68. Woody Holton, *Liberty Is Sweet: The Hidden History of the American Revolution* (New York: Simon & Schuster, 2021), 509.

69. Lefkowitz, 25.

70. O'Donnell, 42.

71. Fischer, 50.

72. Bliven, 97.

73. Ibid., 98.

74. Bliven, 98, and Johnston, *The Battle of Harlem Heights*, 82–83. Bliven estimates the number of American soldiers engaged in the battle at about two thousand; according to Johnston, it was nearly 1,800. Thirty-seven-year-old George Clinton was a veteran of the French and Indian War and served in the New York General Assembly and the Continental Congress. He was appointed a brigadier general of militia by the New York Provincial Congress in December 1775 and a brigadier general in the Continental Army by Congress in March 1777, at which point he held two commissions because the State Convention refused to accept his resignation as brigadier general of militia. Clinton was elected governor of New York in 1777 and held that office for twenty-one years, then served as fourth vice president of the United States (from 1805 to 1812) in the administrations of Thomas Jefferson and James Madison.

75. Bliven, 98.

76. Johnston, *The Battle of Harlem Heights*, 84.

77. Bliven, 98–99.

78. "An Excerpt from the Journal of Lieut. David Dimock," *American Monthly Magazine*, vol. 1 (Washington, DC: National Society Daughters of the American Revolution, July 1892), 353–354.

79. Joseph Reed to Mrs. Reed, September 22, 1776, in Johnston, *The Battle of Harlem Heights*, 138.

80. Bliven, 99.

81. Joseph Reed to Mrs. Reed, September 22, 1776, in Johnston, *The Battle of Harlem Heights*, 138. Tilghman, a graduate of the College of Philadelphia, was a thirty-one-year-old Maryland merchant who had recently joined Washington's staff. Of the thirty-two officers who assisted the commander-in-chief as aides-de-camp during the war, he served with Washington the longest by far, from August 1776 to November 1783.

82. Bliven, 99–100.

83. George Washington to John Hancock, September 18, 1776. *Founders Online*, National Archives. https://founders.archives.gov/documents/Washington/03-06-02-0264.

84. Bliven, 100.

85. Tench Tilghman to James Tilghman, September 19, 1776, in *Memoir of Lieut. Col. Tench Tilghman, Secretary and Aid to Washington, together with an Appendix, con-*

taining Revolutionary Journals and Letters Hitherto Unpublished (Albany, NY: J. Munsell, 1876), 138–139.

86. George Clinton to the New York Convention, September 18, 1776, in Johnston, *The Battle of Harlem Heights*, 141–142.

87. George Clinton to Peter Tappen, September 18, 1776, in ibid., 143–144. It is uncertain whether, or to what extent, American artillery played a role in the battle. A pair of their field pieces may have been deployed in the Hollow Way as George Clinton states, but it is doubtful they would have been dragged up the hill to the buckwheat field. Johnston, *The Battle of Harlem Heights*, 84n1. However, Private Oliver Burnham of Knowlton's Rangers later recalled that the Americans "took two field pieces as they (the British) were dragging them up through a buckwheat field," and perhaps the captured guns were turned on the enemy. Recollections of Oliver Burnham, in Johnston, *The Battle of Harlem Heights*, 179.

88. George Harris to his uncle (date unspecified), in ibid., 207.

89. John Montresor, Journal (date unspecified), in ibid., 223.

90. Loftus Cliffe to "Jack," September 21, 1776 (Loftus Cliffe Papers, William L. Clements Library, University of Michigan), in Hagist, *These Distinguished Corps*, 63.

91. Hessian Account of the Action, in Johnston, *The Battle of Harlem Heights*, 225. Colonel von Donop, forty-four years of age, came from one of Hesse-Cassel's leading noble families and was personal adjutant to Friedrich William II, Landgraf of Hesse-Cassel and head of the Hessian army, who gave von Donop the prestigious command of the Jäger Corps in America. He was mortally wounded at the Battle of Red Bank in 1777.

92. Report of Major C. L. Baurmeister, in ibid., 226.

93. Washington's General Orders, September 17, 1776, in ibid., 162. Letter to John Hancock on September 18 and the New York State Convention on September 23, Johnston, *The Battle of Harlem Heights*, 130 and 133, respectively. "Gallant and brave Col. Knowlton." Ibid., 162.

94. Nathanael Greene to Nicholas Cooke, September 17, 1776, in Showman, 300.

95. Nathanael Greene to William Ellery[?], October 4, 1776, in ibid., 307.

96. George Weedon to John Page, September 20, 1776, in Commager, 471.

97. William Howe to George Germain, September 21, 1776, in Johnston, *The Battle of Harlem Heights*, 204.

98. Loftus Cliffe to "Jack," September 21, 1776 (Loftus Cliffe Papers, William L. Clements Library, University of Michigan), in Atkinson, 397.

99. Account of the Retreat from New York and Affair of Harlem Heights, by Colonel David Humphreys, in Johnston, *The Campaign of 1776 Around New York and Brooklyn*, Part 2:91.

100. David Griffiths to Leven Powel, September 18, 1776, in Johnston, *The Battle of Harlem Heights*, 171–172.

101. Martin, 24–25.

102. Ibid., 25.

103. Johnston, *The Battle of Harlem Heights*, 88.

104. For a partial list of American casualties at Harlem Heights, see Peter Force, *American Archives: consisting of a collection of authentick records, state papers, debates, and letters and other notices of publick affairs, the whole forming a documentary history of the origin and progress of the North American colonies; of the causes and accomplishment of the American revolution; and of the Constitution of government for the United States, to the final ratification thereof; in six series,* vol. 3 (Washington, DC: Prepared and Published Under Authority of an Act of Congress, 1837), 717–722. See also Johnston, *The Battle of Harlem Heights,* 192–193.

105. McCullough, 219.

106. Bliven, 101.

107. Benjamin Trumbull, Journal, September 16, 1776, in Rhodehamel, 224.

108. Gold Silliman to Mrs. Silliman, September 17, 1776, in Johnston, *The Battle of Harlem Heights,* 150.

109. George Clinton to the New York Convention, September 18, 1776, in Ibid., 141. A subaltern was a company-grade officer below the rank of captain, i.e., a lieutenant, ensign, or cornet (the latter being the most junior officer in a cavalry troop and the equivalent of an ensign in an infantry company).

110. Tench Tilghman to James Tilghman, September 19, 1776, in Tilghman, 139.

111. Richards, 26.

112. Stephen Kemble, "Journals of Lieut.-Col. Stephen Kemble," *Collections of the New York Historical Society for the Year 1883* (New York: New York Historical Society, 1884), 89.

113. William Howe to George Germain, September 21, 1776, in Johnston, *The Battle of Harlem Heights,* 204.

114. Report of Major C. L. Baurmeister, in ibid., 226–227.

115. George Harris to his uncle (date unspecified), in ibid., 207–208.

116. John Heinrichs to A. L. Schlozer, in ibid., 227–228.

117. Ketchum, *The Winter Soldiers,* 221–222.

118. Cox, 156.

119. Fischer, 309.

120. Lengel, 149–150.

121. Heath, 53.

122. McCullough, 219–220.

123. Ellis, 152.

124. General Howe's Orders as given in Orderly Book of the Brigade of Guards, September 17, 1776, in Johnston, *The Battle of Harlem Heights,* 209.

125. Schecter, 202.

126. Henry Clinton, *The American Rebellion: Sir Henry Clinton's Narratives of his Campaigns, 1775–1782, with an Appendix of Original Documents,* ed. William B. Wilcox (New Haven, CT: Yale University Press, 1954), 47.

127. Kemble, 89.

128. Captain William G. Evelyn to Mrs. Boscowen, September 24, 1776, in Johnston, *The Battle of Harlem Heights,* 214.

129. Frederick Knowlton stated in his pension application that he was obliged to return home upon his father's death. See Johnston, *The Battle of Harlem Heights,* 192. He was promoted to sergeant but furloughed in order that he could

support his father's family in Ashford. He re-enlisted in 1779 and served seven months in a Connecticut regiment, then enlisted once more in 1781 and served four months in a Massachusetts regiment. Frederick was granted a pension upon his application in 1832 while residing in Ashford and died in 1841 at age eighty.
130. Atkinson, 396.
131. Founders Online, National Archives. https://founders.archives.gov/documents/Washington/05-07-02-0156, note.
132. Washington's General Orders, September 17, 1776, in Johnston, *The Battle of Harlem Heights*, 162.
133. George Washington to John Hancock, September 18, 1776. *Founders Online*, National Archives. https://founders.archives.gov/documents/Washington /03-06-02-0264.
134. Joseph Reed to Mrs. Reed, September 17, 1776, in Johnston, *The Battle of Harlem Heights*, 135.
135. Tench Tilghman to James Tilghman, September 19, 1776, in Tilghman, 138.
136. George Clinton to Peter Tappen, September 21, 1776, in Johnston, *The Battle of Harlem Heights*, 143.
137. Jonathan Trumbull to Joseph Trumbull, September 21, 1776, in Stuart, 275.
138. Recollections of Oliver Burnham, in Johnston, *The Battle of Harlem Heights*, 179.
139. Johnston, *The Battle of Harlem Heights*, 79. On November 25, 1893, the Sons of the Revolution in New York erected a statue of Nathan Hale in City Hall Park and marked certain Revolutionary sites with tablets, including one at 143rd Street and Seventh Avenue as the place where Colonel Knowlton and Major Leitch were buried. The exact spot where each was laid to rest is a matter of conjecture.
140. Heath, 53.
141. Atkinson, 396.
142. Founders Online, National Archives. https://founders.archives.gov/documents/Washington/05-07-02-0156, note. Sarah Leitch's petition was laid before Congress on January 25, 1791, and referred to Secretary of War Henry Knox, who reported on February 15, 1791, in favor of granting the request. The House of Representatives resolved to grant the petition on February 26, but it is unclear whether the resolution was acted upon. On June 30, 1834, Congress resolved to pay "to the legal representatives of the late Margaret Leitch, widow of the late Major Andrew Leitch, a major in the army of the revolution . . . the seven years' half pay" to which "widows and children were entitled by the resolution of Congress of the twenty-fourth of August seventeen hundred and eighty."
143. Cox, 164.
144. Ibid., 197–198.
145. Martin, 54.
146. Ibid., 26.

CHAPTER FOUR: PERSPECTIVE
1. Stephenson, 246.
2. Ferling, 142.

3. Bliven, 103.

4. David Smith, *New York 1776: The Continentals' First Battle* (New York: Osprey Publishing, 2008), 65.

5. Henry Knox to William Knox, September 23, 1776, in Johnston, *The Battle of Harlem Heights*, 150–151.

6. George Washington to John Hancock, September 18, 1776. *Founders Online*, National Archives. https://founders.archives.gov/documents/Washington/03-06-02-0264.

7. Joseph Reed to Mrs. Reed, September 17, 1776, in Johnston, *The Battle of Harlem Heights*, 135.

8. Joseph Reed to Mrs. Reed, September 22, 1776, in ibid., 136–137.

9. Captain John Gooch to Thomas Fayerweather, September 23, 1776, in ibid., 154.

10. Johnston, *The Battle of Harlem Heights*, 98.

11. Ellis, 154–155 and 206n41.

12. Farewell Address to the Army, November 2, 1783, in Washington, *This Glorious Struggle*, 285.

13. Royster, 246–247.

14. Martin, 25.

15. John Jay, "The Battle of Harlem Plains, Oration before the New York Historical Society, September 16, 1876" in *Commemoration of the Battle of Harlem Plains on Its One Hundredth Anniversary by the New York Historical Society, September 16, 1876* (New York: New York Historical Society, 1876), 13.

16. George Washington to John Hancock, November 16, 1776, in Washington, *This Glorious Struggle*, 77. Daniel Knowlton was captured twice during the Revolution and exchanged with other prisoners. The first time, after being taken prisoner at Fort Washington, he spent about two years in captivity, confined for some period aboard the infamous prison ship *Jersey*, and part of the time in an old meetinghouse on Long Island. The second time occurred at the Battle of Horseneck, Connecticut, in December 1780. Daniel rose to the rank of first lieutenant and was stationed at Fort Trumbull in New London, Connecticut, when the war ended. In 1783, he retired to farm life at Ashford, where he died in 1825 at age eighty-six.

17. James Wilkinson, *Memoirs of My Own Times*, vol. 1 (Philadelphia: Abraham Small, 1816. Reprint: Sagwan Press, 2015), 117.

18. James Grant to Johann Rall, December 21, 1776, in William S. Stryker, *The Battles of Trenton and Princeton* (Boston: Houghton, Mifflin, 1898), 334–335.

19. George Washington to Joseph Reed, December 23, 1776, in Washington, *This Glorious Struggle*, 82.

20. George Washington to John Hancock, December 27, 1776, in ibid., 89.

21. George Washington to John Cadwalader, December 27, 1776. *Founders Online*, National Archives. https://founders.archives.gov/documents/Washington/03-07-02-0352

22. Remarks by George Germain, May 3, 1779, in *The Parliamentary Register: Or History of the Proceedings and Debates of the House of Commons during the Fifth Session of the Fourteenth Parliament of Great Britain*, vol. 11 (London: John Stockdale, 1802), 392. https://books.google.com/books?id=ekZFAAAAYAAJ&pg=PA392

&lpg=PA392&dq=All+our+hopes+were+blasted+by+that+affair+at+Trenton.&so
urce=bl&ots=B29fNIJzWY&sig=ACfU3U0z9ihHlzX7wfKXsC5DRXscyaTXOQ&h
l=en&sa=X&ved=2ahUKEwiO1oD6-YfhAhUPh-AKHS4sCYg4ChDo
ATAAegQIChAB#v=o.

23. Ashbel Woodward, 16.

24. Patrick Henry Woodward, 4.

25. Phelps, 134.

26. Acceptance by Governor O. Vincent Coffin, in Patrick Henry Woodward, 8.

27. Historical Address by P. Henry Woodward, in ibid., 9 and 40.

28. "Knowlton Award." Military Intelligence Corps Association. https://www.
mica-national.org/awards/knowlton-award/.

29. Hon. Samuel Utley, in Knowlton Association of America, 45.

30. Ashbel Woodward, 15–16.

31. Hon. Samuel Utley, in Knowlton Association of America, 45.

32. "Kin Honors Connecticut Patriot—Thomas Knowlton," *Connecticut Bicentennial Gazette* 5, no. 1 (December/January 1776), 3.

33. One can be forgiven for questioning why the Connecticut General Assembly designated Hale as the state's sole official hero in 1985 and thereby consigned his superior officer to relative obscurity. Notwithstanding Hale's unquestioned bravery and commitment to the Revolution, what he accomplished in its service pales beside Knowlton's record. A dispassionate consideration of the respective contributions by these two martyrs to the Patriot cause can yield only one conclusion: there is simply and emphatically no comparison between them. Replacing one man with the other as the official state hero at this point would presumably be problematic for some, but at the very least Colonel Knowlton deserves equal billing with Captain Hale. Why not have a pair of state heroes? As they were connected in life, so let them be for eternity—at least in Connecticut. Partisans of Israel Putnam clearly have a case to make for their man, but the argument for Knowlton and Hale rests on their having made the ultimate sacrifice for the cause in which all three were engaged.

Bibliography

CORRESPONDENCE, DIARIES, JOURNALS, MANUSCRIPT SOURCES, AND MEMOIRS

Adams Papers. *Founders Online*. National Archives.

Anderson, Enoch. *Personal Recollections of Captain Enoch Anderson*. Wilmington: Historical Society of Delaware, 1896. Reprint: New York Times and Arno Press, 1971.

Bangs, Isaac. *Journal of Lieutenant Isaac Bangs, April 1 to July 29, 1776*. Edward Bangs, ed. Cambridge, MA: John Wilson and Son, 1890.

Benedict, Erastus C. *The Battle of Harlem Heights, September 16, 1776, Read before the New York Historical Society, February 5, 1878, with a Preface and Notes*. New York: A. S. Barnes & Co., 1880.

Clinton, Sir Henry. *The American Rebellion: Sir Henry Clinton's Narratives of his Campaigns, 1775–1782, with an Appendix of Original Documents*. William B. Willcox, ed. New Haven, CT: Yale University Press, 1954.

Commager, Henry Steele, and Richard B. Morris, eds. *The Spirit of 'Seventy–Six: The Story of the American Revolution as Told by Participants*. New York: Harper & Row, 1967.

Commemoration of the Battle of Harlem Plains on Its One Hundredth Anniversary by the New York Historical Society, September 16, 1876. New York: New York Historical Society, 1876.

Connecticut Historical Society. *Orderly Book and Journals Kept By Connecticut Men While Taking Part in the American Revolution, 1775–1778.* Hartford, CT: Connecticut Historical Society, 1899.

———. *Rolls of Connecticut Men in the French and Indian War.* Vol. 1, 1755–1757. Hartford, CT: Connecticut Historical Society, 1903.

———. *Rolls of Connecticut Men in the French and Indian War.* Vol. 2, 1758–1762. Hartford, CT: Connecticut Historical Society, 1905.

———. *Rolls and Lists of Connecticut Men in the Revolution, 1775–1783.* Hartford, CT: Connecticut Historical Society, 1901.

Dann, John C., ed. *The Revolution Remembered: Eyewitness Accounts of the War for Independence.* Chicago: University of Chicago Press, 1980.

Force, Peter. *American Archives: Consisting of a collection of authentick records, state papers, debates, and letters and other notices of publick affairs, the whole forming a documentary history of the origin and progress of the North American colonies; of the causes and accomplishment of the American revolution; and of the Constitution of government for the United States, to the final ratification thereof; in six series.* Washington, DC: Prepared and Published Under Authority of an Act of Congress, 1837.

Heath, William. *Memoirs of Major-General William Heath.* William Abbatt, ed. New York: William Abbatt, 1901. Reprint: Sagwan Press, 2015.

Howe, William. *The Narrative of Lieut. Gen. Sir William Howe, in a Committee of the House of Commons, on the 29th of April, 1779, Relative to His Conduct, during His Late Command of the King's Troops in North America: To which are added some Observations upon a Pamphlet, entitled Letters to a Nobleman.* London: H. Baldwin, 1780. Reprint: Toronto Public Library.

Johnston, Henry P., ed. *Record of Connecticut Men in the Military and Naval Service during the War of the Revolution, 1775–1783.* Adjutant-General's Office. Hartford, CT: Case, Lockwood & Brainard Co., 1889. https://www.americanwars.org/ct-american-revolution/knowltons-rangers-1776.htm.

Journal and Correspondence of the Council of Safety of Maryland, 1776–1777. Archives of Maryland Online, Vol. 12. https://msa.maryland.gov/megafile/msa/speccol/sc2900/sc2908/000001/000012/html/am12—1.html.

Kemble, Stephen. "Journals of Lieut.-Col. Stephen Kemble." *Collections of the New York Historical Society for the Year 1883.* New York: New York Historical Society, 1884.

Martin, Joseph Plumb. *Memoir of a Revolutionary Soldier: The Narrative of Joseph Plumb Martin.* Mineola, NY: Dover Publications, 2006.

Massachusetts Historical Society. Documents from its collection of personal accounts and eyewitness descriptions contained in its web exhibition on the Battle of Bunker Hill, 2003. http://www.mass hist.org/bh/index.html.

National Archives. NARA M804. *Case Files of Pension and Bounty-Land Warrant Applications Based on Revolutionary War Service, compiled ca. 1800 – ca. 1912, documenting the period ca. 1775 – ca. 1900.* Catalog ID 300022.

New York Historical Society. *Commemoration of the Battle of Harlem Plains on Its One Hundredth Anniversary by the New York Historical Society, September 16, 1876.* New York: New York Historical Society, 1876.

The Parliamentary Register: Or History of the Proceedings and Debates of the House of Commons during the Fifth Session of the Fourteenth Parliament of Great Britain. Vol. 11. London: John Stockdale, 1802.

"Rare Signature of America's First Head of Military Intelligence." *Between the Covers Rare Books Catalog 211: Americana Part II.* [BTC#413461]. Between the Covers Rare Books, 2017, 26–27. https://www.betweenthecovers.com/images/upload/c211.pdf.

Reed, William B. *Life and Correspondence of Joseph Reed, Military Secretary of Washington at Cambridge; Adjutant-General of the Continental Army; Member of the Congress of the United States; and President of the Executive Council of the State of Pennsylvania.* Vol. 1. Philadelphia: Lindsay and Blakiston, 1847. Reprint: Adamant Media Corporation, 2006.

Rhodehamel, John, ed. *The American Revolution: Writings from the War of Independence, 1775–1783.* New York: Library of America, 2001.

Richards, Samuel. *Diary of Captain Samuel Richards: Connecticut Line, Revolutionary War 1775–1781.* Published by his great-grandson, 1909. Reprint: Big Byte Books, 2014.

Rodney, Caesar. *Letters to and from Caesar Rodney, 1756–1784,* George Herbert Ryden, ed. Philadelphia: Historical Society of Philadelphia, 1933.

Rogers, Robert. *Journals of Major Robert Rogers: Containing an Account of the Several Excursions He Made under the Generals Who Commanded upon the Continent of North America during the Late War; from Which May be Collected the Most Material Circumstances of Every Campaign upon That Continent, from the Commencement to the Conclusion of the War; with an Introduction and Notes, and an Appendix Containing Numerous Documents and Papers relating to the Doings of Major Rogers While Commanding at Michilimackinack, in 1767; and His Conduct in the Early Part of the Revolutionary War. By Franklin B. Hough.* Albany, NY: Joel Munsell's Sons, 1883.

Scheer, George F., and Hugh F. Rankin. *Rebels and Redcoats: The American Revolution Through the Eyes of Those Who Fought and Lived It.* New York: Da Capo Press, 1987.

Seymour, George Dudley, ed. *Documentary Life of Nathan Hale, Comprising All Available Official and Private Documents Bearing on the Life of The Patriot, Together with an Appendix, showing the background of his life; including his family circle; his college friends; his friends made as a school-master and in the army; with many illustrations, portraits and buildings that knew his footsteps.* New Haven, CT: Privately printed, 1941.

Showman, Richard K., ed. *The Papers of General Nathanael Greene.* Vol. 1, December 1766—December 1776. Published for the Rhode Island Historical Society. Chapel Hill: University of North Carolina Press, 1976.

Taylor, C. James, Margaret A. Hogan, Celeste Walker, Anne Decker Cecere, Gregg L. Lint, Hobson Woodward, and Mary T. Claffey, eds. *The Adams Papers,* Adams Family Correspondence. Vol. 7, January 1786–February 1787. Cambridge, MA: Harvard University Press, 2005.

Taylor, Robert J., ed. *The Adams Papers,* Papers of John Adams. Cambridge, MA: Harvard University Press, 1979.

Thacher, James. *A Military Journal During the American Revolutionary War, from 1775 to 1783, Describing Interesting Events and Transactions of This Period, with Numerous Historical Facts and Anecdotes, from the Original Manuscript.* Boston: Richardson and Lord, 1823.

Tilghman, Tench. *Memoir of Lieut. Col. Tench Tilghman, Secretary and Aid to Washington, together with an Appendix, containing Revolutionary Journals and Letters Hitherto Unpublished.* Albany, NY: J. Munsell, 1876.

Tomlinson, Abraham, ed. *The Military Journals of Two Private Soldiers, 1758–1775, together with Numerous Illustrative Notes to Which is Added, a Supplement, Containing Official Papers on the Skirmishes at Lexington and Concord.* Poughkeepsie, NY: Abraham Tomlinson, 1855.

Trumbull, John. *Autobiography, Reminiscences and Letters of John Trumbull, from 1756 to 1841.* New York: Wiley and Putnam, 1841.

———. *The Autobiography of Colonel John Trumbull: Patriot-Artist, 1756–1843.* Theodore Sizer, ed. New Haven, CT: Yale University Press, 1953.

Washington, George. *The Diaries of George Washington.* Vol. 3. Donald Jackson, ed. Charlottesville: University Press of Virginia, 1978.

———. *The Papers of George Washington*, Colonial Series. Vol. 2. W.W. Abbot, ed. Charlottesville: University Press of Virginia, 1983.

———. *The Papers of George Washington*, Revolutionary War Series. Vol. 3. Philander D. Chase, ed. Charlottesville: University Press of Virginia, 1988.

———. *The Papers of George Washington*, Revolutionary War Series. Vol. 6. Philander D. Chase and Frank E. Grizzard, Jr., ed. Charlottesville: University Press of Virginia, 1994.

———. *The Papers of George Washington*, Revolutionary War Series. Vol. 7. Philander D. Chase, ed. Charlottesville: University Press of Virginia, 1997.

———. *The Papers of George Washington*, Presidential Series. Vol. 7. Jack D. Warren, Jr., ed. Charlottesville: University Press of Virginia, 1998.

———. *This Glorious Struggle: George Washington's Revolutionary War Letters.* Edward G. Lengel, ed. Charlottesville: University Press of Virginia, 2007.

———. *The Writings of George Washington from the Original Manuscript Sources.* Vol. 6. Electronic Text Center, University of Virginia Library. https://web.archive.org/web/20110218172145/http://etext.lib.virginia.edu/etcbin/toccer-new2?id=WasFi06.xml&images=images/modeng&data=/texts/english/modeng/parsed&tag=public&part=16&division=div1#n0052-20.

Wilkinson, James. *Memoirs of My Own Times.* Vol. 1. Philadelphia: Abraham Small, 1816. Reprint: Sagwan Press, 2015.

PUBLISHED SECONDARY SOURCES

Anderson, Fred. *Crucible of War: The Seven Years' War and the Fate of Empire in British North America, 1754–1766.* New York: Vintage Books, 2000.

Atkinson, Rick. *The British Are Coming: The War for America, Lexington to Princeton, 1775- 1777.* New York: Henry Holt, 2019.

Bakeless, John. *Turncoats, Traitors and Heroes: Espionage in the American Revolution.* New York: Da Capo Press, 1998.

Baker, Mark Allen. *Spies of Revolutionary Connecticut: From Benedict Arnold to Nathan Hale.* Charleston, SC: History Press, 2014.

Bayles, Richard M. *History of Windham County, Connecticut.* New York: W. W. Preston & Co., 1889.

Beck, Derek W. *Igniting the American Revolution, 1773–1775.* Naperville, IL: Sourcebooks, 2015.

———. *The War Before Independence, 1775–1776.* Naperville, IL: Sourcebooks, 2016.

Berkin, Carol. *Revolutionary Mothers: Women and the Struggle for America's Independence.* New York: Alfred A. Knopf, 2005.

Billias, George Athan, ed. *George Washington's Generals.* New York: William Morrow, 1964.

———. *George Washington's Opponents: British Generals and Admirals in the American Revolution.* New York: William Morrow, 1969.

Bliven, Jr., Bruce. *Battle for Manhattan.* New York: Henry Holt, 1956. Reprint: Literary Licensing, 2012.

Borneman, Walter R. *American Spring: Lexington, Concord, and the Road to Revolution.* New York: Little, Brown, 2014.

Carbone, Gerald M. *Washington: Lessons in Leadership.* New York: Palgrave Macmillan, 2010.

Chernow, Ron. *Washington: A Life.* New York: Penguin Press, 2010.

Coffin, Charles. *The Lives and Services of Major General John Thomas, Colonel Thomas Knowlton, Colonel Alexander Scammell, Major General Henry Dearborn, compiled by Charles Coffin.* New York: Egbert, Hovey & King, Printers, 1845. Reprint: Wentworth Press, 2019.

Cox, Caroline. *A Proper Sense of Honor: Service and Sacrifice in George Washington's Army.* Chapel Hill: University of North Carolina Press, 2004.

Cremin, Lawrence A. *American Education: The Colonial Experience, 1607–1783.* New York: Harper & Row, 1972.

Crowdy, Terry. *The Enemy Within: A History of Espionage*. New York: Osprey Publishing, 2006.

Cuneo, John R. *Robert Rogers of the Rangers*. New York: Richardson & Steirman, 1987.

Daniels, Bruce C. "Economic Development in Colonial and Revolutionary Connecticut: An Overview." *William and Mary Quarterly* 37, no. 3 (July 1980), 429–450.

Daughters of the American Revolution. *American Monthly Magazine*. Vol. 1 (Washington, DC: National Society Daughters of the American Revolution, July 1892).

Drake, Francis S. *Life and Correspondence of Henry Knox, Major-General in the American Revolutionary Army*. Boston: Samuel G. Drake, 1873.

Ellis, Joseph J. *Revolutionary Summer: The Birth of American Independence*. New York: Alfred A. Knopf, 2013.

Ferling, John. *Almost a Miracle: The American Victory in the War of Independence*. New York: Oxford University Press, 2007.

Field, Thomas W. *The Battle of Long Island*. Brooklyn, NY: Long Island Historical Society, 1869.

Fischer, David Hackett. *Washington's Crossing*. New York: Oxford University Press, 2004.

Fleming, Thomas. *Liberty! The American Revolution*. New York: Viking, 1997.

Frothingham, Richard, Jr. *History of the Siege of Boston, and of the Battles of Lexington, Concord, and Bunker Hill*. Boston: Little, Brown, 1873.

Gallagher, John J. *The Battle of Brooklyn, 1776*. New York: Da Capo Press, 1995.

Hagist, Don N. *Noble Volunteers: The British Soldiers Who Fought the American Revolution*. Yardley, PA: Westholme, 2020.

———. *These Distinguished Corps: British Grenadier and Light Infantry Battalions in the American Revolution*. Warwick, UK: Helion, 2021.

Higginbotham, Don. *George Washington and the American Military Tradition*. Athens: University of Georgia Press, 1985.

Holton, Woody. *Liberty Is Sweet: The Hidden History of the American Revolution*. New York: Simon & Schuster, 2021.

Hoock, Holger. *Scars of Independence: America's Violent Birth*. New York: Crown, 2017.

Hubbard, Robert Ernest. *Major General Israel Putnam: Hero of the American Revolution*. Jefferson, NC: McFarland, 2017.

Humphreys, Col. David. *An Essay on the Life of the Honourable Major General Israel Putnam. Addressed to the State Society of the Cincinnati in the State of Connecticut. And first published by their order.* Boston: Samuel Avery, 1818.

Johnston, Henry P. *The Battle of Harlem Heights, September 16, 1776; With a Review of the Events of the Campaign.* New York: Macmillan, 1897. Reprint: Franklin Classics, 2018.

———. *The Campaign of 1776 Around New York and Brooklyn. Including a New and Circumstantial Account of the Battle of Long Island and the Loss of New York, with a Review of Events to the Close of the Year.* Brooklyn, NY: Long Island Historical Society, 1878.

Ketchum, Richard M. *Decisive Day: The Battle for Bunker Hill.* Garden City, NY: Doubleday, 1974.

———. *The Winter Soldiers.* Garden City, NY: Doubleday, 1973.

Kidder, William L. *The Revolutionary World of a Free Black Man: Jacob Francis, 1754–1836.* S.p., 2021.

"Kin Honors Connecticut Patriot—Thomas Knowlton." *Connecticut Bicentennial Gazette* 5, no. 1 (December 1775/January 1776), 3.

Knowlton Association of America, Miner Rockwell Knowlton, and William Herrick Griffith. *Prospectus and Year Book Containing the History, Constitutions, By-laws, List of Officers and Members of the Knowlton Association of America From Its Organization, with an Account of the First and Second Reunions.* Albany, NY: S. H. Wentworth, printer, 1897.

Lefkowitz, Arthur S. *Eyewitness Images from the American Revolution.* Gretna, LA: Pelican, 2017.

Lengel, Edward G. *General George Washington: A Military Life.* New York: Random House, 2005.

MacMillan, Margaret. *War: How Conflict Shaped Us.* New York: Random House, 2020.

McCullough, David. *1776.* New York: Simon & Schuster, 2005.

Merriam, John M. "The Military Record of Brigadier General John Nixon of Massachusetts." *Proceedings of the American Antiquarian Society at the Semi-Annual Meeting Held in Boston, April 14, 1926.* Vol. 36, Part 1 (Worcester, MA: American Antiquarian Society, 1926), 38–70.

Middlekauff, Robert. *The Glorious Cause: The American Revolution, 1763–1789.* New York: Oxford University Press, 2005.

———. *Washington's Revolution: The Making of America's First Leader.* New York: Alfred A. Knopf, 2015.

Miller, Nathan. *Spying for America: The Hidden History of U.S. Intelligence.* New York: Dell, 1989.

Morgan, Jr., W.F. "Army Intelligence Heritage Series: LTC Thomas Knowlton Biography and Sources Revisited." *The Vanguard.* Journal of the Military Intelligence Corps Association 15, no. 2 (April 2010), 14–23.

O'Donnell, Patrick K. *Washington's Immortals: The Untold Story of an Elite Regiment Who Changed the Course of the Revolution.* New York: Atlantic Monthly Press, 2016.

O'Shaughnessy, Andrew Jackson. *The Men Who Lost America: British Leadership, the American Revolution, and the Fate of the Empire.* New Haven, CT: Yale University Press, 2013.

Palmer, Dave Richard. *The Way of the Fox: American Strategy in the War for America, 1775–1783.* Westport, CT: Greenwood Press, 1975.

Perley, Sidney. "Colonel Thomas Knowlton." *Historical Collections of the Essex Institute* 58, no. 2 (April 1922), 89–100. https://archive. org/stream/essexinstitutehi58esseuoft/essexinstitutehi58esseuoft_djvu.txt.

Phelps, M. William. *Nathan Hale: The Life and Death of America's First Spy.* New York: Thomas Dunne Books, 2008.

Philbrick, Nathaniel. *Bunker Hill: A City, A Siege, A Revolution.* New York: Viking, 2013.

———. *Valiant Ambition: George Washington, Benedict Arnold, and the Fate of the American Revolution.* New York: Viking, 2016.

Price, David. "Thomas Knowlton's Revolution." *Journal of the American Revolution.* September 2, 2021. https://allthingsliberty.com/2021/09/thomas-knowltons-revolution/.

Rose, Alexander. *Washington's Spies: The Story of America's First Spy Ring.* New York: Bantam Books, 2014.

Royster, Charles. *A Revolutionary People at War: The Continental Army and American Character, 1775–1783.* Published for the Institute of Early American History and Culture, Williamsburg, VA. Chapel Hill: University of North Carolina Press, 1979.

Savas, Theodore P., and J. David Dameron. *A Guide to the Battles of the American Revolution.* El Dorado Hills, CA: Savas Beatie, 2013.

Schecter, Barnet. *The Battle for New York: The City at the Heart of the American Revolution.* New York: Walker, 2002.

Schenawolf, Harry. "Battle of Harlem Heights Sept. 16, 1776: Americans Gave the British a Good Drubbing." *Revolutionary War Journal.* January 15, 2014. https://www.revolutionarywarjournal.com/battle-of-harlem-heights/.

———. "Forgotten Warrior of the American Revolutionary War: Colonel Thomas Knowlton." *Revolutionary War Journal.* August 25, 2015. https://www.revolutionarywarjournal.com/thomas-knowlton/.

Shepherd, Joshua. "'Cursedly Thrashed': The Battle of Harlem Heights." *Journal of the American Revolution.* April 15, 2014. https://allthingsliberty.com/2014/04/cursedly-thrashed-the-battle-of-harlem-heights/.

Shepherd, William R. *The Battle of Harlem Heights.* New York: G. P. Putnam's Sons, 1898.

Smith, David. *New York 1776: The Continentals' First Battle.* New York: Osprey, 2008.

Spring, Matthew. *With Zeal and with Bayonets Only: The British Army on Campaign in North America, 1775–1783.* Norman: University of Oklahoma Press, 2008.

Staiti, Paul. *Of Arms and Artists: The American Revolution Through Painters' Eyes.* New York: Bloomsbury Press, 2016.

Stephenson, Michael. *Patriot Battles: How the War of Independence Was Fought.* New York: Harper Perennial, 2008.

Stiles, Henry R. *History of the City of Brooklyn, N.Y.* Vol. 1. Brooklyn, NY: Published by Subscription, 1867.

Stocking, Rev. Charles Henry Wright, D.D. *The History and Genealogy of the Knowltons of England and America.* Vol. 1. New York: Knickerbocker Press, 1897. Reprint: Wentworth Press, 2016.

Stryker, William S. *The Battles of Trenton and Princeton.* Boston: Houghton, Mifflin, 1898.

Stuart, I. W. *Life of Jonathan Trumbull, Sen., Governor of Connecticut.* Boston: Crocker and Brewster, 1859. Reprint: Kessinger, 2010.

Symonds, Craig. L. *A Battlefield Atlas of the American Revolution.* El Dorado Hills, CA: Savas Beatie, 2018.

Taylor, Alan. *American Revolutions: A Continental History, 1750–1804.* New York: W. W. Norton, 2016.

Van Buskirk, Judith L. *Standing in Their Own Light: African American Patriots in the American Revolution.* Norman: University of Oklahoma Press, 2017.

Ward, Christopher L. *The Delaware Continentals, 1776–1783.* Wilmington: Historical Society of Delaware, 1941.

Wood, Gordon S. *The Radicalism of the American Revolution.* New York: Alfred A. Knopf, 1992.

Woodward, Ashbel. *Memoir of Col. Thomas Knowlton, of Ashford, Connecticut.* Boston: Henry W. Dutton & Son, 1861. Reprint: Andesite Press, 2015.

Woodward, Patrick Henry. *Statue of Colonel Thomas Knowlton: Ceremonies at the Unveiling.* Hartford, CT: Press of the Case, Lockwood & Brainard Company, 1895. Reprint: Franklin Classics, 2018.

Wright, Jr., Robert K. *The Continental Army.* Washington, D.C.: U.S. Army Center of Military History, 1983.

MISCELLANEOUS

"American Wars." *Knowlton's Rangers, 1776.* https://www.americanwars.org/ct-american-revolution/knowltons-rangers-1776.htm.

"Ashford." ConnecticutHistory.org. https://connecticuthistory.org/towns-page/ashford/.

"George Washington's Mount Vernon." *Battle of Harlem Heights.* Fred W. Smith National Library for the Study of George Washington at Mount Vernon. https://www.mountvernon.org/library/digitalhistory/digital-encyclopedia/article/battle-of-harlem-heights/.

"Knowlton Award." Military Intelligence Corps Association. https://www.mica- national.org/awards/knowlton-award/.

"Lt. Col. Thomas Knowlton, Connecticut's Forgotten Hero." Connecticut Society of the Sons of the American Revolution. https://www.connecticutstar.org/lt-col-thomas-knowlton-connecticuts-forgotten-hero/.

Pelland, Dave. "Colonel Thomas Knowlton Monument, Hartford." CT Monuments.net: Connecticut History in Granite and Bronze. October 21, 2013. http://ctmonuments.net/2013/10/colonel-thomas-knowlton-monument-hartford/.

"September 16: Lt. Col. Thomas Knowlton Dies a Hero's Death at the Battle of Harlem Heights." Today in Connecticut History, Office of the State Historian. September 16, 2019. https://todayinc-thistory.com/2019/09/16/september-16-lt-col-thomas-knowlton-killed-at-the-battle-of-harlem-heights/.

"Thomas Knowlton: A Small Town's National Hero." Connecti-cutHistory.org. September 16, 2020. https://connecticuthistory.org/thomas-knowlton-a-small-towns-national-hero/.

(Note: All websites listed were accessed from July 2021 through April 2022.)

Acknowledgments

THE VIEWS EXPRESSED IN THIS NARRATIVE are mine alone, unless specifically attributed to another author or historical account, and I assume full responsibility for its content. Notwithstanding that, the assistance of others in this endeavor is deeply appreciated, and I would like to thank the following: Bruce H. Franklin, publisher at Westholme Publishing, for inviting me to pursue this undertaking and guiding it through to completion; Mark Edward Lender and James Kirby Martin, distinguished historians and editors of the *Small Battles* series sponsored by Westholme that includes this volume, for their scholarly guidance; Don N. Hagist, author and managing editor of the *Journal of the American Revolution*, for sharing information from his research about British grenadiers and light infantry in the Revolution for his latest book; manuscript editor Noreen O'Connor-Abel for her eagle eye and laudable efficiency; Roger S. Williams, publisher of my first three books and literary mentor, for encouraging me to consider this project; Jennifer Martin, Executive Director of The Friends of Washington Crossing Park (FWCP), for being a supportive boss; Elena Peters, Collections Associate at the Connecticut Historical Society, for her efforts on my behalf to secure information about Thomas Knowlton; friend and fellow author Larry Kidder for inspiring me with his recent work about Jacob Francis, a free Black man and former indentured servant who at age twenty-two fought at Harlem Heights with Colonel Paul Dudley Sargent's 16th Continental Regiment from Massachusetts, which supplied several officers for Knowlton's Rangers; authors Glenn Williams and Kim Burdick along with Bill Welsch of the American Revolution Round Table (ARRT) of Richmond and Tom McAndrew of the ARRT of Philadelphia for various technical corrections to the manuscript; Thomas Maddock II, FWCP historical interpreter, for being a mentor and sounding board; and, last but not least, my wife Alison for encouraging my literary pursuits and tolerating my erratic mood swings. Each in their own way has facilitated this enterprise.

Index